THE I.R.S.
vs.
THE MIDDLE CLASS

Other Books by the same Author:

Milton and Servetus
The Theory of Logical Expression
The Modernity of Milton
The Plaster Saint
The Religion of the Occident
Wanton Sinner
Church Wealth and Business Income
The Essene Heritage
The Great Tax Fraud
The Churches: Their Riches, Revenues, and Immunities
Praise the Lord for Tax Exemption
When Parochial Schools Close
Tax Revolt: U.S.A!
Tax Rebellion, U.S.A.
The Federal Reserve and Our Manipulated Dollar
The Religious Empire
The Story of Christian Origins
How to Defend Yourself Against the
    Internal Revenue Service
The Essence of Jefferson
How to Establish a Trust and Reduce Taxation
The Essene-Christian Faith
How You Can Save Money on Your Taxes
The Continuing Tax Rebellion

THE I.R.S.

versus

THE MIDDLE CLASS

or

How the Average Citizen
Can Protect Himself
from the
Federal Tax Collector

by

Martin A. Larson

THE DEVIN-ADAIR COMPANY, PUBLISHERS
Old Greenwich, Conn. 06870

For information address The Devin-Adair Company, 143 Sound Beach Avenue, Old Greenwich, Connecticut 06870.

Library of Congress Catalog Card Number: 79-67271
ISBN: 0-8159-5824-2

Manufactured in the United States of America

Second Printing   February   1981

CONTENTS

What This Book Tells You:

1. How to communicate with the Internal Revenue Service when it calls or writes stating that your income-tax returns are to be audited.

2. How arrangements should be made for any such conference.

3. What to do in preparation for such a meeting or confrontation.

4. How to protect your documents — checkbooks, deposit slips, information concerning property transfers, and any other kind of financial data.

5. How to compel the IRS to furnish you with a Bill of Particulars.

6. How to conduct yourself at what we call the "cooperative" audit — that is, one in which deductions, expenditures, and other reports contained in the 1040 are verified.

7. What techniques you should follow if you insist on having witnesses present and using a tape-recorder at the Conference.

8. What steps to follow in the administrative process if you refuse to permit an examination of documents at a first conference.

9. How to appeal to the Conferee in the District Office, to the Appellate Division, and to the Tax Court.

10. How to appeal to the Circuit Court of Appeals.

11. How to utilize tax-shelters and loopholes in the Code for the purpose of avoiding a large portion and possibly all of your federal income taxes.

12. How to avoid the traps, snares, and pitfalls planted in the Code, by which thousands of honest businessmen have been seriously injured or ruined utterly.

13. How to use the Privacy Act for your protection.

14. How to prevent your estate from being drastically reduced by probate costs and by estate and inheritance taxes.

15. How to use a variety of court decisions — given in the Appendix — for your defense.

AND MORE, MORE, MUCH MORE!

Introduction

More and more Americans are finding that the federal income tax and the Internal Revenue Service are threatening to devour them, and this is especially true of the Middle Class producers. Furthermore, the statute under which it operates cannot be enforced without violating several of the most sacred provisions in our Bill of Rights. Nor is this all: it is filled with loopholes and exclusions which enable favored corporations and individuals to avoid all, or most, of the taxes imposed on others; and, even worse, it is filled with irrational traps and snares which can be used to destroy those hard working independents who attempt to create an estate or a competence for themselves.

The fact is that the Internal Revenue Service has harassed, oppressed, impoverished, or destroyed uncounted numbers of completely honest citizens. The primary purpose of the federal income tax is not so much to collect revenue as it is to control and regiment the people; an alternative tax could be imposed which would be fair to everyone, produce the same revenue at far less cost to our citizens; but this would take from the politicians and the bureaucrats the power to confer favors upon some to purchase their policial support and to destroy others who might otherwise become effective opponents.

We estimate that not less than thirty million living Americans have suffered at the hands of the Internal Revenue Service; and this situation has engendered a widespread rebellion, which can no longer be entirely ignored or concealed by the media. It has also forced the Congress to enact certain laws which, when understood and utilized, enable taxpayers to defend themselves more successfully than was previously possible.

There is no doubt that whenever a taxpayer is forced to disgorge money which he does not believe is owing following an audit, the federal government has created resentment which will continue to smolder in the heart of the victim as long as he lives. It is no accident or misnomer that the IRS is called the American Gestapo; for it has, with a vengeance, fulfilled the predictions made March 3, 1910, by Richard E. Byrd, then Speaker of the Virginia House of Delegates and grandfather of the present Senator Harry F. Byrd. This Amendment, he declared, "means that the state actually invites the Federal government to invade the territory to oust its jurisdiction and to establish Federal dominion within the innermost citadel of reserved right ... It will extend the Federal power so as to reach the citizen in the ordinary business of life. A hand from Washington will be stretched out and placed upon every man's business; the eye of the Federal inspector will be in every man's counting house.

"The law of necessity will have inquisitorial features; it will provide penalties. It will create a complicated machinery.

"Under it, business will be hauled into courts distant from their business.

"Heavy fines imposed by distant and unfamiliar tribunals will constantly menace the taxpayers.

"An army of Federal inspectors, spies, and detectives will descend upon the state. They will compel men of business to show their books and disclose the secrets of their affairs. They will require statements and affidavits ... the inspector can blackmail the taxpayer ...

"When the Federal government gets this stranglehold on the individual businessman, state lines will exist nowhere but on the maps. Its agents will everywhere supervise the commercial life of the states ...."

Every year, the Internal Revenue Service conducts about three million audits, from which it collects billions of dollars. The point is that much of this would never be paid if the taxpayers knew how to protect themselves; for a great deal of it is obtained by false interpretations of the Code, or by sheer bluff, since the victims do not understand the law, do not take the time to study it themselves, or cannot afford reliable counsel. Furthermore, a lawyer or even a CPA, who might charge $500 to $1,000 to contest a small amount, might prove of little value or help; and an appeal to the Tax Court or to the Circuit Court of Appeals with the help of a lawyer will normally run into many thousands of dollars.

I can testify from personal experience how terrible a battle with the IRS can be. My first was in 1945-46, when, to the best of my knowledge and belief, I had paid every penny of taxes due. I was ordered to appear at the Agency headquarters with all books, records, cancelled checks, etc. (which they kept for almost two years); and when I obeyed this summons, I was informed that they *knew* that I had fraudulently avoided or evaded $45,000 in taxes and that, before they were through with me, they would seize everything I owned (about $150,000 in real estate) and, in addition, send me to prison. (Remember that this was during the period when almost every Internal Revenue Service agent was being enriched by soliciting and receiving bribes.) After a two-year battle, I was signally victorious; but I made a vow that if ever I could do anything to force this Agency to operate with some degree of decency and justice, I would do so; and now, for many years, I have been engaged in the attempt to fulfill that oath.

If we had statesmen instead of politicians in Congress, they would immediately put an end to inflation by discharging at least one million federal bureaucrats, cutting the federal budget by fifty per cent, eliminating the income tax on every kind of production — individual and corporate — , liquidating the national debt, turning all so-called welfare programs over to the states, replacing the Federal Reserve Act with a constitutional monetary system and a solid currency, abolishing all subsidies to private organizations, and terminating the Social Security System in favor of mandatory personal trusts.

Do we find any of those with access to the means of mass-communication making such proposals? Not at all — quite the contrary. Our leaders are attempting to solve our economic problems with vast programs of deficit spending, which is like pouring gasoline into a fire. Enormous debts have been and are being created for future generations to pay, or to be repudiated outright, or to be liquidated with worthless currency. Unemployment is to be reduced by putting more people on the federal payroll!

I agree with Jefferson that the federal government should pursue only those activities specifically enumerated in ARTICLE I, Section 8, of the Constitution. So limited, the General Government would automatically reduce its budget by more than fifty per cent and enable it to meet its expenditures without either a personal or a corporate income tax. The replacement of Social Security by a Universal Trust System could save another $100 billion. Even should we admit that almost its present level of expenditures is mandatory, it could obtain the necessary revenue by replacing its income taxes with a five per cent general transactions tax, which would cost the people only about one-third in terms of what the federal treasury receives.

Thomas Jefferson warned again and again that it is the nature of all central government to become a despotism, seeking to control and regiment every member of its constituency; and he added that the means used to accomplish this objective consists in the creation of a huge national debt; heavy taxation; and finally a great centralized bureaucracy, with progressively greater and more diversified power.

We are deeply concerned over the problems of all productive citizens, whether self-employed or working for wages or salaries. However, we are especially concerned over those of the great middle-class, those twenty millions or more (perhaps forty-five millions, including spouses and adult children) who, to a greater or lesser extent, are in business for themselves, keep their own books, and are responsible for their own economic welfare and survival. It is, first, because they tend to think for themselves and thus constitute the backbone of any republican form of government; without them, our nation would already have degenerated into a totally authoritarian state. Since they cannot be adequately policed or their incomes accurately determined; and since they ask no favor from government and desire only to be left alone, they are the natural enemies of the bureaucracy. It is no accident that the IR Code is studded with traps and snares used to oppress or destroy them; and the battle between them continues to rage unabated.

History and observation demonstrate that bureaucracies and central governments entertain a deep hostility toward free-enterprise independents; however, this is the socio-economic group which alone makes a republican and responsible form of government possible. Despotisms enter into partnerships with the rich and the powerful; on the other hand, slaves, serfs, peasants, and wage-workers can almost always be controlled. To a considerable degree, the well-paid managerial class belong, as their executive administrators, with the ruling elite. Wage-workers and most salaried employees receive their periodic pay, from which has already been subtracted their social security, union dues, state and federal income taxes, and other deductions: in general, they notice only the bottom line — THE TAKE-HOME PAY, which does not derive from investment and does not depend on any decisions of their own.

Entirely different is the situation of the self-employed. They must make their own investments; keep their own books; and, after earning their money, share a large portion of it with an authority from which they receive nothing specific in return except harassment and more extortion.

This has set the stage for the conflict which is now raging between them and the Internal Revenue Service. In this battle, however, the Middle Class is in a strategic position, because the bureaucrats have never been able to devise a method by which to collect taxes on Middle Class incomes before they are received; nor do they know any method by which to determine accurately just what such incomes are.

If we are to save this nation and the republican form of government in the western world, the Middle Class must learn how to protect itself.

This book is therefore dedicated especially to the survival, growth, and prosperity of this group. Incidentally, it is also dedicated to the ideals of constitutional government and the sovereign rights of the American people.

Martin A. Larson

Addendum

Since many do not clearly understand their immunities and exemptions under the Internal Revenue laws, the following information seems *apropos*, and it refers to the schedules in force during 1979-80:

No federal income tax is due nor is any return required when the following incomes are received from wages or salaries and deductions are not itemized on returns; each dependant and taxpayer is entitled to an exemption of $1,000; and automatic deductions ranging from $1,700 for married persons filing separately and $2,300 for single persons and heads of households and $3,400 for spouses filing jointly are permitted. There is no tax on income received in the form of Social Security.

	No Added Exemptions	With Five Dependants	With Ten Dependants
Single person	$3,300	$ 8,300	$13,300
Single person over 65	4,300	9,300	14,300
Married persons filing jointly	5,400	10,400	15,400
A married person filing separately	2,700	7,700	12,700
Married persons over 65 filing jointly	7,400	12,400	17,400
A married person over 65 filing separately	3,700	8,700	13,400

We suggest that all persons earning wages or salaries file a Form W-4 with their employers showing a number of exemptions and allowances (the latter worth $750 each) sufficient so that over-withholding will not occur. If no tax was due for the previous year and if none is expected to be due during the present one, the employee may write Exempt on Line 3 of the W-4 Form, and then the employer will not withhold any income tax.

Although no tax may be due, a return is required from individuals who not only report exemptions but who also itemize allowances on their returns for interest, taxes, charitable contributions, medical expenses, etc. However, because of legal and additional allowances, a very substantial income may be entirely exempt not only from taxation, but also from withholding; and they can qualify the employee to file the W-4 Form with the word *Exempt* on Line 3 thereof.

Note the following, which shows the amount of income that may be received without tax-liability:

	With Five Dependants Plus Ten Allowances	With Five Dependants Plus Twenty Allowances
Single person	$14,000	$21,500
Couple with one income	15,250	22,750

If incomes consist entirely of wages or salaries, which are subject to Social Security and/or income-tax withholding, these amounts may be received without any requirement for filing an income-tax return.

IMPORTANT REVISIONS
IN THE INTERNAL REVENUE CODE
contained in the
REVENUE ACT OF 1978

The Revenue Act of 1978 included 171 proposed changes, emanating either from the Ways and Means Committee of the House or the Senate Finance Committee. Of these, 135 were adopted in some form. The Conference Report, dated October 15, which became law when the President signed it, contains 311 pages. The following are the most important provisions which are of greatest general interest.

LARGER AUTOMATIC DEDUCTIONS

Section 1 is amended to increase the statutory amount of income exempt from taxation (in addition to personal exemptions) from: $3,200 to $3,400 for spouses filing joint returns;
$2,200 to $2,300 for single persons and heads of households;
$1,600 to $1,700 for married persons filing separately.

In addition, the tax brackets are widened and reduced in number from 25 to 15, except for single persons, who have 16.

INCREASE IN PERSONAL EXEMPTIONS

Section 151 is amended to increase the personal exemption from $750 to $1,000, which means that no return is required from

Single persons or heads of households with income of	$3,300.00
Single persons or heads of households over 65	4,300.00
Spouses filing jointly	5,400.00
Spouses over 65 filing jointly	7,400.00
Married persons filing separately	2,700.00
Married persons over 65 filing separately	3,700.00

OFFSETTING TAX INCREASES

Section 42 of the Code, however — which permitted a deduction of $35.00 for each person covered in a return or a 2 per cent deduction from Adjusted Gross Income not exceeding $180.00 — HAS BEEN DELETED: AS HAS Section 164(a)(5), which permitted deductions for local taxes paid on the purchase of gasoline and petroleum products for personal use. As a result, very little or no reduction in income taxes will result from the increase in personal exemptions and the slight increase in automatic deductions for those who do not itemize.

CORPORATION INCOME TAXES REDUCED

Section 11 is amended in order to effect the following changes in corporate income taxation:

RATES ON TAXABLE INCOME

Previous	New
First $25,000 at 20%	First $25,000 at 17%
Second $25,000 at 22%	Second $25,000 at 20%
All over $50,000 .... 48%	Third $25,000 at 30%
	Fourth $25,000 at 40%
	All over $100,000 .... 46%

TERMINATION OF THE
ALTERNATIVE CAPITAL GAINS TAX

Section 1201 is amended by deleting subsections (b) and (c), which provided for the alternative tax on capital gains; which is to say that taxpayers will no longer have the option of paying a capital gains tax of 25 per cent on the entire amount of gain or the regular rate on one-half of such gain.

REDUCTION IN CAPITAL GAINS TAX
FOR NON-CORPORATE TAXPAYERS

Section 1202 is amended so that for all non-corporate taxpayers 60 per cent of capital gains will not be taxed and the remaining 40 per cent will be taxed as ordinary income. The 60 per cent will be excluded from preference income, but the 40 per cent — whenever this exceeds $10,000 for most taxpayers — will be subject to the preference income tax on such excess. That is, if the capital gains total $30,000, $12,000 will be subject to the ordinary tax; and of this, the tax on $2,000 will be subject to an additional tax of 15 per cent.

EXAMPLES OF NON-CORPORATE
CAPITAL GAINS TAXATION
ON $60,000 FOR TAXPAYERS
NOW IN 30% BRACKET
(formerly 50%)

Previous to January 1, 1979		Following January 1, 1979	
Capital Gains Tax...	$15,000.00	Taxable	$24,000.00
Preference Tax on		Tax at 30%	7,200.00
$50,000 or 15 per		Preference Tax	
cent of $12,500 ...	1,875.00	on $14,000	2,100.00
Total	$16,875.00	Total	$9,300.00

The new rate schedules, therefore, will mean a savings of $7,375 for this taxpayer.

TAX ON $25,000 OF CAPITAL GAINS FOR
A TAXPAYER IN THE 20% BRACKET

Previous to January 1, 1979		Following January 1, 1979	
Capital Gains Tax ...	$2,500.00	20% of $10,000	$2,000.00
Preference Tax	450.00		
Total	$2,950.00	Total	$2,000.00

This taxpayer would therefore save $950.00.

REDUCTION IN CORPORATE INCOME TAX

Section 1201(a)(2) is amended by reducing the alternative tax on capital gains for corporations from thirty to twenty-eight per cent.

EXCLUSION FROM TAXATION ON INCREASED GAINS FROM THE SALE OF CERTAIN HOMES

Section 121 (a) and (b) is amended so that any taxpayer — an individual or a married couple — having attained the age of 55 and having been domiciled in a residence for three of the previous five years, may now sell the same for $100,000 more than is invested therein and be immune to taxation on the gain. Such gain shall not be treated as preference income. However, the immunity shall apply only once in a lifetime.

If there is a "rollover," that is, if a new home is acquired within 18 months, the sale does not affect the immunity on a subsequent sale. Furthermore, the once-in-a-lifetime rules does not apply if the sale of a home is necessitated by removal to a new location in order to obtain regular employment.

NEW LAW IN REGARD TO REPORTING INCOME FROM TIPS

Section 6001 is amended so that no employer need keep records of tips paid to employees except those paid in charge receipts and copies of statements made by employees to the employer. There need be no reporting of tips by the employer. The amended provision requires no one except the recipient of them to report them to the IRS.

THE CONFIRMED STATUS OF CONTRACT EMPLOYEES

A new section (numbered only as 530 in the Revenue Act of 1978 but not yet printed in the 1979 Internal Revenue Code) is extremely important because it makes the attainment of self-employment or contractual status far easier than it has been in the past.

The new law states that if the taxpayer-employer does not treat an individual as an employee (i.e., if he does treat him or her as a contract-employee) before January 1, 1980, and if all required returns are made and taxes paid by such individual on the basis of a self-employed, independent contractor, then such individual shall be deemed not to be an employee for tax purposes. Furthermore, the IRS is prohibited from issuing any regulation or Revenue Ruling in regard to this matter before January 1, 1980.

The importance of this provision can scarcely be overestimated. It means that millions of individuals can now attain the status of self-employed persons; that anyone who has any reasonable claim to such status will be so treated by the government for FICA and tax reporting purposes if he is so treated by his employer before January 1, 1980, and if he makes all reports and pays all taxes required by such status during 1979. Furthermore, the IRS may not issue any regulation or ruling which could imperil or invalidate the status of such self-employed or contractual employees during the year 1979.

JEFFERSON'S CREED AND DECLARATION OF FAITH

Let us, then, with courage and confidence pursue our own federal and republican principles . . . — a wise and frugal government, which shall restrain men from injuring one another, which shall leave them otherwise free to regulate their own pursuits of industry and improvement, and shall not take from the mouth of labor the bread it has earned. This is the sum of good government, and this is necessary to close the circle of our felicities . . . . . .

I deem the essential principles of our government [to be] Equal and exact justice to all men, of whatever state or persuasion, religious or political; peace, commerce, and honest friendship with all nations — entangling alliances with none; the support of the State governments in all their rights, as the most competent administrations for our domestic concerns and the surest bulwarks against anti-republican tendencies . . . the supremacy of the civil over the military authority; economy in the public expense, that labor may be lightly burdened; the honest payment of our debts and sacred preservation of the public faith; encouragement of agriculture and of commerce . . . . ; the diffusion of information and the arraignment of all abuses at the bar of public reason; freedom of religion; freedom of the press; freedom of the person under the protection of *habeas corpus;* and trial by juries impartially selected — these principles form the bright constellation which has gone before us, and guided our steps through an age of revolution and reformation. The wisdom of our sages and the blood of our heroes have been devoted to their attainment. They should be our creed and our political faith — the text of civil instruction — the touchstone by which to try the services of those we trust [with political office]; and should we wander from them in moments of error or alarm, let us hasten to retrace our steps and to regain the road which alone leads to peace, liberty, and safety.

First Inaugural Address, March 4, 1801

One The Middle Class: Definition and Importance

This handbook focusses especially upon the problems of the great American middle class in relation to the Internal Revenue Service; and first, let us briefly define what we mean by this segment of society.

Broadly conceived, it comprises those who earn a decent living or have retired in some degree of comfort on savings accumulated during many years of productive service or on annuities deriving therefrom. Although none can live in luxury by means of inherited wealth or exercise personal political power, all of them stand above the poverty level. They are, furthermore, those who work or have worked regularly, received reasonable compensation, pay the bulk of the taxes, support their own families, place their surplus in savings and loan associations or other investments, make no serious trouble or expense for the police, and constitute the responsible citizenry of the nation. Taken as a whole, they total nearly sixty per cent of our population, as well as the real base on which our culture and civilization rest. In 1975, out of 82,177,000 returns — of which 20,424,000 paid no income tax — 36,016,000 had adjusted gross incomes ranging from $10,000 to $50,000, with a mean of about $18,000. In a total Adjusted Gross Income of $948.1 billion, theirs was $657.6 billion or 69.4 per cent. Of taxable income totalling $590.9 billion, theirs was $444.9 billion, or 75.3 per cent, on which they paid $87.1 billion — or 70 per cent of the total. In addition, they and their employers contributed an estimated $55 billion to the Social Security system, which means that the average combined income and SS taxes in this group were about $4,000, or 22.2 per cent of their incomes for these levies alone.[A]

More specifically, however, and technically, the Middle Class may be defined as consisting of those members of society who are engaged in some form of self-employment: proprietorships, farming, commission selling, the professions, individual contracting, etc. Between 1945 and 1974, individual proprietorships increased from 5,589,000 to 10,874,648. In addition, there were 1,062,000 partnerships; almost 2 million small corporations; and millions of other independents engaged in business, all of them deriving their incomes from the general public. All of these keep their own books and records; none have revenues subject to income or Social Security withholding; their total income runs into the hundreds of billions (which we will discuss more in detail in another chapter). These people are responsible for their own welfare and success: because they must make correct decisions in order to survive economically, they are likely to think independently in the political sphere also. The IRS regards them with resentment because they cannot be adequately policed nor can their incomes be accurately determined. These are the people who make the operation of republican government possible. Had it not been for the fact that this class had previously arisen in England, Germany, France, the Netherlands, and Scandinavia, the republican revolutions which took place there between 1500 and 1850 could not have occurred. Were it not for this class in America, the Constitution we have could never have emerged; and were it not for its continued existence, this nation would soon degenerate into a totalitarian state or a communist dictatorship, precisely as happened in various countries which had no well-developed Middle Class.

In various ways, the Roosevelt administration did everything in its power to impoverish or even eliminate the middle class; and to do likewise has always been a prime objective of every overgrown central government, the reason being that its members cannot be completely controlled through regimentation. It is therefore no accident that the IR Code is literally filled with traps and snares so cleverly embedded that very few — even including lawyers and CPAs — are aware of their existence. Through long experience and personal observation, it has become obvious to me that it is almost impossible for any small independent — no matter how honest — to achieve success and economic security without one or more confrontations with the IRS, during which irrational pitfalls are utilized to impoverish or destroy. And so while the victims imagine themselves secure in the knowledge of their own honesty, they often discover too late that their very honesty has become the road to their ruin.

Business independents should therefore be forewarned and forearmed. We should note, however, that the snares and traps in the Code are counterbalanced by loopholes placed there under pressure from the rich and powerful to enable them legally to avoid much or all taxation. If a Paul Getty can have a personal income of $70 million and pay only $6,000 in income taxation, why should a small businessman or woman, who labors endless hours, pay perhaps half of all net earnings in taxes and be in constant danger of destruction or heavy unexpected assessments because of some unknown provision in the Code, which is written precisely so that it will be beyond the comprehension of any individual, no matter how learned or knowledgeable.

Nevertheless, we can assure the reader that with proper warning and preparation, the members of the middle class can not only avoid the traps in the Code, but can also utilize some of its loopholes; and, by so doing, not only survive, but become comparatively affluent.

We should note, furthermore, that there are millions of managers, technicians, and highly skilled workers in all fields of endeavor who, although their incomes are subject at the source to income and Social Security withholding, are nevertheless potential allies for the independent middle class. Many of these have incomes exceeding those of most independents; both are not only subject to heavy taxation, but can expect little sympathy from the federal government. Their general resentment may kindle into a conflagration upon realizing that about half of the personal federal income tax paid by the American people is used simply to maintain a bureaucracy of 2,500,000, who pay out most of the remainder in the form of favors to induce other parasites to support a system of waste and extortion which defies comprehension.

As we contemplate the enormous burden of federal income

and Social Security taxes, we are appalled that Congress permits their continuance. During the Twenties, the cost of federal operation did not exceed $1 billion, of which not more than one-third was necessary to maintain its payroll. In 1979-80, the federal budget is about $535 billion; the cost of the bureaucracy is nearly $70 billion; the appropriations to operate the Internal Revenue Service alone is about $3 billion and the estimated cost to the citizens of making out their returns and fighting the Service is at least an equal amount.

But this is only the tip of the iceberg. Consider this: the personal and federal income taxes cost the taxpayers approximately three times as much as the government collects; since the money is taken from producers at the point of production, this becomes a built-in element of cost; it must, therefore, be added to the price of goods and services, and will be paid a second time by the producers in their role as consumers. Thus it is obvious that each dollar of revenue received by the Treasury costs the worker two dollars. However, even this is not the whole story: for as goods proceed through the channels of production and distribution, all elements of original cost escalate. Thus, every dollar transmitted by the productive corporation to the Treasury in the form of income or Social Security taxes increases by two dollars the cost of goods when they reach the consumers.

Every dollar paid by corporations in their own income taxes is simply passed on in double measure to the ultimate users. Corporations, therefore, pay no taxes: for these are merely added to costs in the form of higher prices.

There is also another extremely important consideration: since all taxes must be added to basic cost and since this escalates, American goods have become non-competitive in almost all foreign markets and, to a very large extent, even in our domestic. Untold billions of American capital have consequently fled to foreign countries where the multi-nationals construct plants which disgorge their niagaras of merchandise sold everywhere in the world, including the United States. In short, the federal income tax has driven such vast sums of capital abroad that at least four or five million Americans have lost their jobs.

Why are American streets filled with cars built in Germany,

Japan, Italy, Sweden, France, etc? In most of these countries, much government income derives from what is called the value-added tax, but, since this is not imposed on goods going into export, a Volkswagen costs hundreds of dollars less in Michigan than in Germany.

We can demonstrate that after a huge chunk of the producer's as well as the employer's income is taken from them, everything sold in the marketplace costs at least thirty per cent more because of the federal taxes imposed since 1934. Our central government, which spends at least $300 billion for goods and services, could save $100 billion or more merely by terminating its own direct taxes. And its bureaucrats could enjoy the same living standard while receiving thirty per cent less in pay.

Let us note how federal tax exactions affect an independent contractor in 1979 or 1980 who has one helper and who agrees to paint a building for $1,000 (Social Security levies are scheduled to rise sharply during the next few years):

Total cost of job		$1,000.00
For contractor		700.00
For helper		300.00
Income taxes:		
Contractor's, 25%	$175.00	
Helper's, 20%	60.00	
Social Security taxes:		
Contractor's, 8.1%	56.70	
Helper's, 6.05%	18.15	
Contractor's contribution	18.15	
TOTAL		328.00
Remaining for workers		672.00

Thus, 32.5% goes immediately in direct taxes to the federal government, in addition to which there will be various contributions to other levels of government.

However, even this is by no means all: remember that everything these men must purchase to maintain their business and support their families costs thirty per cent more than it would were it not for these federal taxes. In short, were these eliminated, this contractor and his helper could enjoy the same living standard by doing the $1,000.00 job for $450.00.

Consider, then, the general effect of federal taxation: if the taxes imposed since 1933 were eliminated — even with present inflation — the $50,000 house would sell for $35,000 and the $5,000 car would be available for $3,500.

It is obvious that taxes fall most heavily upon the middle or producing classes. Corporations simply pass on their taxes to consumers in the form of higher prices; and the cost of Social Security, levied upon the first $16,500 of earned income, is $1,336.50 in 1978 for the self-employed and $1,996.50 on wages and salaries, half of which is paid by the employers. These sums are scheduled to rise sharply under the Social Security Act of 1977 and will exceed $6,000 in 1985. Meanwhile, tens of billions received in the form of interest, annuities, rentals, royalties, dividends, capital gains, and various other forms of income are immune to SS taxation; much of these are exempt from federal income taxation also; and some are even immune to disclosure.

THE TRUE PURPOSE OF THE INTERNAL REVENUE TAX AND CODE

Why, then, is this system tolerated? Why does Congress continue it? The reasons are as simple as they are indefensible: all the tax-exempts, such as foundations and so-called charities, as well as the individuals who pay little or nothing are avidly in favor of the *status quo* because they are vastly enriched by it; and for this reason they use some of their immune revenues to underwrite the political campaigns of congressmen, who have nothing but contempt for voters who refuse to become politically informed. Lawyers and tax-counsellors make fabulous fees helping clients avoid taxation. And, since the federal government has now developed into a vast system of control and regimentation, this would have to be completely reconstructed if an equitable and constitutional system of taxation were to replace the one which now exists.

When a political entity, an educational institution, a church, or even a so-called charity or research center accepts funds from the federal government or from a tax-free foundation, this becomes a narcotic, far worse than morphine. Since bureaucrats are well aware of this, they almost fall on their knees begging school administrators, colleges, and other ideology-creating institutions to accept government largesse. Once they do so, they are bound hand and foot to the bureaucracy. If such organizations permit any serious dissidence to develop within their domains, the subsidy may be withdrawn. If this deprivation is not sufficient, all exemptions provided in the Code may be terminated and they could be treated as corporations-for-profit; subjected to the most harrowing audits; valid deductions could be disallowed; and levies assessed which could not possibly be paid.

Since almost every church, college, university, school, or charity enjoys various advantages from the government, they now exist as vassals of the super-state. Even if a college refuses to accept a grant or even a loan from the federal government, it may still find itself subject to control. Hillsdale College in Michigan had never accepted a dime from the government; nevertheless, because a few of its students had received private loans guaranteed by a federal agency, it was declared a "recipient institution," subject to a regimentation which it could escape only by expelling such students or providing them with other loans.

Since the IRS can and does exercise such powers, it is obvious that its purpose is not primarily to collect taxes, but to create an authoritarian and conforming society. And it is indeed ironic that in the implementation of such policies, the financing is done by the very people thus reduced to economic servitude.

Even the Post Office has become an important instrument for enforcing discrimination; those who qualify for favors can send their mail for very little, while those who wish to avoid federal control must pay the rates charged the general public. Taxpayers subsidize the Post Office with nearly $2 billion a year to make this system possible.

In the meantime, it is incumbent upon the members of the middle class to protect themselves and to grow in numbers, income, knowledge, assets, and organizations so that the ideals of our Founding Fathers and particularly those of Thomas Jefferson may once again become an honored and dominating force in our nation.

A. Statistics from 1977 *Statistical Abstract*, pp. 258-260.

Two

Lawyers and Certified Public Accountants

Every year the government promises to reform and simplify the tax laws so that it will be easier for the average individual to prepare his own return; however, as if it were preordained in the stars, they are made more complex, and written in language even more incomprehensible. This makes it possible for more parasites to obtain higher fees and for IRS agents to levy heavier assessments by misinterpreting the Code.

All this, however, works for the benefit of the rich and the super-rich, for to them fees of $10,000 or more paid to tax experts constitute comparatively small outlays. Thus the very complexity of the Code, far beyond the comprehension of most bureaucrats, can be used by wily tax-experts to baffle and defeat the government. Some twenty years ago, I met a private counsellor who did the investing and the tax work for several of the most famous stars in Hollywood; he had never lost a battle with the IRS; his own emoluments were fantastic; and his clients paid almost no taxes on annual multi-million-dollar incomes. Discovering this, my previous sympathy for people in the 91 per cent bracket suddenly cooled precipitately and I learned for the first time that these confiscatory tax-rates are intended only for the naive who believe that government documents actually mean what they seem to say. And I concluded that a $40,000-government bureaucrat is no match for a private expert who can make ten times as much or more by defeating him in defense of the very rich.

I remember the occasion on which I had delivered an address advocating a drastic simplification of the Code to be accomplished by eliminating all special deductions, allowances, exclusions, etc.; by giving all taxpayers standard exemptions equal to the cost of living; and then by imposing a much reduced tax-rate on all net income received by corporations, and upon individuals above a cost-of-living allowance. When I concluded, a gentleman approached who stated that my proposal would have tragic consequences; for such simplification would enable everyone to determine his own tax-liability with ease; eliminate the need for literally tens of thousands of federal employees; and, worst of all, reduce almost to nothing, his own present income of $100,000, earned by aiding and abetting wealthy clients to reduce or escape taxation.

About the same time, in 1969, the chairman of the board of one of the larger banks in New York City called me; after identifying himself, he explained that he had paid $104,000 in personal income taxes the previous year; that he had come across my book, *The Great Tax Fraud*, by accident; that it had alerted him to the possibilities, of which he had previously been unaware; that, as a result, he had retained expert counsel and would not be paying one penny of the $140,000 during the current year which he would have paid had he not discovered my book.

I learned that a certain corporation against which the IRS had assessed a deficiency of $33 million, settled for $1 million, after a long-drawn-out battle, in which a private lawyer persuaded the government that this was all it could get; and then he obtained a fee in the same amount. Question: was the $33 million or the $1 million actually due? was there any real liability at all?

However, such expertise is not available to the middle-class taxpayer, who must toil endless hours to operate his business and whose annual income would not be sufficient to satisfy an elite tax-counsellor for a few days of his time. A second-rate attorney expects from $70 to $100 an hour; and almost in the twinkling of an eye, his client may discover that he owes several thousand dollars. Although CPAs have somewhat less exalted notions concerning their value, they can be expensive enough to ruin the small businessman.

This book is written for the specific purpose of enabling middle-class taxpayers to do their own research, prepare their own briefs and other documents, and conduct their own defense before the IRS. And here I may perhaps be forgiven for pointing out, as a result of personal experience, that this is entirely possible and practical. In 1962, when my knowledge of the IRS, its procedures, and its Code and laws, was comparatively vestigial, I was able to win a complete victory. After the agent had assessed a deficiency of $24,000 (which was upheld by the Conferee in the District Office) because of a trap in which I had been enmeshed, I first sought out a man reputed to be an excellent CPA; however, when I discovered that he was actually a worse enemy than the government agent, I released him, and presented my problem to a tax-attorney, said to be the most competent and successful in the city. He demanded an advance fee of $2,000 in order to do the preliminary research; and added that he would expect a substantial portion of any amount that he could save me by "negotiation." I then decided to do my own research, which consumed a week; and to write my own brief, which I completed in two days. After I went to the Appellate Division, I not only paid no tax, but collected $38,500 from the Internal Revenue Service as a result of a provision in the Code of which I had before known nothing. Even more important, I found that I had become involved in another trap, but from which I was able to extricate myself; had I not done so, I might have been reduced to almost complete penury.

There is scarcely any situation so dangerous or precarious for the middle-class taxpayer as that in which he seeks aid from a lawyer or a CPA and places total confidence in him to defend him against the IRS. I have found that both stand in terror of this government agency. Although members of the bar declare that they have an absolute right to practice before the IRS and to represent a taxpayer, no matter what the situation, I have known various cases in which dissidents find it virtually impossible to find a reputable lawyer who will defend them: and if one does so, the "defense" has sometimes been a plea for conviction rather than acquittal. Even if an honest, competent, and conscientious lawyer may not face imminent disbarment for offering a vigorous and effective defense, there are ways in which the government can so harass and injure him that he will under no circumstances undertake the defense of a person who wishes to make a constitutional defense against the IRS.

CPAs are even more timorous than lawyers when facing the IRS. In order to represent a taxpayer in a dispute with the IRS, he must be certified by the agency; and decertification will normally involve a drastic reduction of income. In any confrontation with the IRS, therefore, he will be extremely cautious, for under no circumstances will he risk the loss of an employment which pays up to $100 an hour.

Since most lawyers and CPAs charge such fees for services which may prove of little or no value, the middle-class taxpayer should approach them, if at all, with the greatest diffidence. It certainly seems absurd to pay one of these $1,000 or more in a dispute involving a smaller sum of money. Many taxpayers have paid assessments of hundreds of dollars, year after year, of which only a portion or none at all may have been due, simply because it was simpler, easier, and cheaper than to hire competent and reliable counsel for defense.

However, every taxpayer should realize that when he signs a consent-assessment, he has set himself up as an annual target for audits. Senator Barry Goldwater told me that he had been audited eight years in succession and that it had cost him $8,000 one year to prove that he did not owe anything. The Honorable J. Bracken Lee, former governor of Utah and mayor of Salt Lake City, was audited annually for thirty-five years, and every year paid several hundred dollars. Finally, however, when a huge deficiency was assessed against him in 1971, he refused to pay; and, after a long battle, received a refund of $13.72. Since then, the IRS has left him alone.

The middle-class taxpayer should realize that before a CPA or lawyer can represent him, he must be entrusted with power-of-attorney, a requirement imposed by the Inquisition during the Middle Ages. This means that the person representing the taxpayer can make any deal he sees fit with the IRS — including the total betrayal or destruction of his client. In a typical case, the IRS. In order to represent a taxpayer in a dispute of any kind, he must be certified by the agency; and decertification will normconsiderable time and research might be required to invalidate the claim, and since the potential fee does not justify such effort, the CPA or lawyer reaches the conference table with little or none of the preparation necessary for victory at the Appellate level.

In this ritual, the taxpayer's representative will probably point out two or three of the most indefensible disallowances on which the $2,000.00 assessment is based. With seeming reluctance and a great show of generosity, the Conferee agrees to restore those deductions. When an agreement is reached, perhaps the CPA will obtain a reduction of $800.00 and then charge the taxpayer $500.00 for his services. A member of the bar may persuade the Conferee to reduce the assessment by $1,200 and then charge $800 for his greater expertise.

Even while charging such fees, the lawyer or CPA is likely to undertake the defense of a small businessman with indifference. After all, clients come and go, but the IRS, with which they must constantly deal, goes on and on; in addition to which it has awesome powers of retaliation against anyone upon whom it seeks revenge. The lawyer and the CPA are interested principally in their fees and they generally seek, at all costs, to avoid enmity with the IRS. Experience and observation indicate that in ordinary cases, the lawyer does not defend his client either with vigor or perserverance.

Middle-class taxpayers should understand that while *they* must compete in the open market against all comers and, in order to survive or prosper, must offer satisfactory goods or services at reasonable prices, this is not the situation with a lawyer, or even a CPA. Since they must obtain certain credentials in order to operate, they seek to eliminate competitors. They practice under a strict closed-shop system; since they have a monopoly, they charge unrestricted monopoly prices, which are the most the traffic will bear. They do not need many clients or very much work, for a very small number may suffice for a munificent income. Although there are notable exceptions in this as in every profession, thousands of lawyers lounge in their offices until some client, who may pay thousands of dollars for a few days of dilatory attention, walks in. A lawyer may charge $2,000.00 for some simple document which his stenographer can prepare in an hour or two.

In order to protect their monopoly, this profession has developed a jargon of its own, which a layman is never supposed to
understand. These are the people who, as politicians, make our
laws and establish the rules under which all others must live. I
have heard federal judges threaten citizens with contempt of
court and imprisonment for trying to quote the Constitution,
which these same judges have taken a solemn oath to uphold and
maintain against all comers without mental reservation. Is it
necessary for a person to spend seven or eight years in a law
school and twenty years in the practice of law, in order that he
may subvert the Constitution which our Founding Fathers gave
us in words so simple that no child can misunderstand them?

There is nothing that lawyers would love more dearly than
the power to send every citizen to prison who even tries to fill out
any semi-legal document himself. They would like to force every
citizen to pay $500 for filling out a simple form, which a typist can
complete in ten minutes. A banker — who was also a graduate of
a good law school — once told me that he could easily complete a
simple trust indenture in an hour or two, but would be breaking
the law by so doing: instead, I would have to pay a licensed
attorney $1,000 for this unwanted service.

I once listened to a federal judge threaten to send a defendant to prison for insisting on defending himself in court; however, since then, the Supreme Court has established — in *Faretta
v. California*, 422 U.S. 806, decided June 30, 1975 — that every
citizen has this absolute right; it declared further that no defendant need accept the services of an unwanted, court-appointed
attorney; and it even implied that, since the Constitution declares
that every person is entitled to counsel, such defense is not
limited to licensed members of the bar. *Faretta* also points out
that in several of the American colonies, no lawyer was permitted
to represent anyone in court for a fee.

What we are stressing for the average middle-class taxpayer
is the extreme importance — and even more the possibility — of
adequate and successful self-defense in all confrontations with
the Internal Revenue Service, even up to and including the Tax
Court. If millions, or at least tens of thousands, of American
citizens would follow the suggestions offered in the succeeding

chapters, we could soon put an end to the present system of taxation and re-establish the federal government on the basis of the
Constitution.

Having said all the preceding we wish to add that this does
not apply by any means to all lawyers or CPAs. I have met several
who are reasonable, competent, conscientious, and deeply
sympathetic with the embattled taxpayer. I have even met some
who are willing to stake their entire careers for what they consider truth and justice. Some have been disbarred because of
their battles for honesty and equity. Some of the noblest men in
our history, including Thomas Jefferson, were educated and
trained for the practice of law. May that type of lawyer increase
in numbers and influence; and may they be rewarded in terms
other than mere money or political office for their efforts in
defense of justice and the common man.

Three   The IRS Operation

A GENERAL WARNING

As already noted, the IR Code is filled with unsuspected pitfalls which have been used to destroy or impoverish completely honest, hardworking individuals; and, in addition, IRS personnel constantly utilizes gray areas in the law — perhaps intentionally so written, in order to make questionable interpretations and consequent assessments not legally authorized. It is indeed ironic that the federal government should operate what is called the Small Business Administration, which costs the taxpayers several hundred million dollars a year, ostensibly to help establish such enterprise, while, at the same time, using the IRS to destroy countless numbers who would succeed were it not for government persecution.

On two occasions the IRS threatened my destruction; although the battles were difficult and harrowing, I was able to survive economically because of careful study and determined resistance. However, had I then been in possession of a book like this one, I would not have been subject to the uncertainty and terror which became my lot for long periods of time. But I have known others — some of whose experiences will be summarized in this chapter for the instruction of the reader — who were not so fortunate, but who could have escaped danger with proper foreknowledge.

Perhaps the most significant warning that should be given the average middle-class taxpayer is that he should place little faith in any statement made by an IRS agent. Whether he speaks from deceit or ignorance is irrelevant. Remember that whereas it is a felony for a taxpayer to make a misstatement to an IRS official, *he* can never be held responsible or accountable for anything he says or does. Section 7214 of the Code provides that if he KNOWINGLY demands money not due or more money than is due, he is subject to a prison term of five years, a fine of $10,000, dismissal from the Service, and the requirement that he make summary restitution; however, court records reflect no case in which this law has been enforced — although violated millions of times — except in the case of agents who solicit bribes and who, in return for these, have enabled evaders to escape taxation. Are we therefore to conclude that the only individuals who can plead immunity because of ignorance of the law are those employed by the government at enormous cost to administer it?

When, therefore, the middle-class taxpayer faces an assessment, he has three choices: first, to hire counsel so expensive and/or so unreliable that it may well lead to ruin; second, to rely on what the IRS says, which is even more dangerous; or, third, to study the law and defend himself in order to avoid destruction or heavy assessments.

In order to illustrate what taxpayers can and should do, the remainder of this chapter is devoted to thumb-nail sketches of actual case-histories, all of which are factual and typical of thousands of others. Each embodies an object-lesson, indicating how some taxpayers could have defended themselves successfully and what others actually have done to avoid tragedy.

A.   THE ENTRAPMENT CYCLE

(1)   The Man Who Traded One Building for Another

One man who owned an unencumbered apartment project traded this for another of the same value, on which there was a mortgage of $50,000.00. When he inquired from the IRS whether he might later be involved in any tax-liability, he was told to seek private counsel and that the government would determine in due course whether any tax was due. When he suggested that if the IRS could make such a decision at a time when corrective action would be impossible, it should be able to do so at once, he was ordered out of the office. Several "experts," including a professor of income-tax law at a local university, explained that since he was trading like for like, there would be no tax-liability. When the transaction was completed, deeds were exchanged and he received a certified check in the amount of $50,000.00, which he used forthwith to pay off the mortgage.

Three years later, the IRS audited his return, and declared that the $50,000.00 was taxable "boot," on which — since local tax lawyers agreed with the IRS — he paid a capital gains tax of $12,500, in addition to interest and penalties. However, research later revealed that no tax was actually due under Section 1031(b) of the Code. The money was therefore collected illegally, largely because the so-called experts agreed that the IRS levy was legal. Everyone agreed that had no cash been involved in the deal, there could not have been any tax; yet the statute states explicitly that there can be no tax-liability in such a transaction unless there is a gain: and how can the assumption of a debt constitute a gain?

Interestingly enough, this writer has been trying for years to make the IRS declare officially whether or not such a transaction involves any possible tax-liability; and, in spite of the fact that several long letters have been received, the Agency refuses to say whether or not such is the case.

The lesson here is that before consummating any transaction, neither the IRS nor the so-called "experts" should be trusted. Had the man in this case studied the law himself, he would have required the other party to the transaction to pay off the mortgage previous to its consummation; or he might have defended himself successfully even in the situation which ensued.

(2) Selling a Shopping Center or Other Property

One man, after completing a shopping center, became so worn out from worry and overexertion that he was desperate to sell on whatever terms he could. He therefore agreed to accept $400,000 for a property which had cost him $500,000. He found a buyer who would pay this amount provided he would accept $375,000 in cash and a piece of vacant land valued at $25,000.00. The transaction was completed on this basis.

When the IRS audited his return, it declared that he owed a

tax of $93,750 on a transaction on which his actual loss was
$100,000. This and other incredible demands drove him to a study
of the IR Code, its laws, traps, and loopholes. He then discovered
that his $100,000 loss was not a capital, but an operating, loss,
which would entitle him to a possible refund of all taxes paid
during the three previous years, as well as to a remission of all
levies due during the current and in five succeeding years.

However, the trap in which he had become enmeshed caused
him nightmares and untold loss of sleep, until he discovered that
if he could dispose of the vacant land during the current fiscal
year, he would not only escape the proposed IRS levy, but would
also be eligible to refunds and tax-remissions totalling more than
$50,000. He therefore sold the land for about $20,000; and, by so
doing, reaped an advantage totalling nearly $150,000.00,
compared to the situation in which he would otherwise have
found himself.

(3) Entrapment in an Individual Real-Estate Corporation

A certain man who owned an apartment building decided for
certain reason to organize an individually owned corporation, to
which he deeded his property. Later, this entity acquired several
other buildings at different dates.

However, about fifteen years later, it became necessary to
liquidate his holdings. One of the assets had been depreciated for
the full period and had only a small basis; others still had an
undepreciated base of 70 or 80 per cent.

He now discovered that in order to dissovle the corporation
and transfer the properties to himself, he would have to do so, not
at the value of their equities, but at their present and inflated
market prices. Although the 16th Amendment provides that
under its authority, only incomes may be taxed, the IRS Code
requires that in such dissolutions and transfers — even though
no income is involved — the entire difference between the value
of the original stock and the present market value of the
properties shall be taxed as capital gain.

Had all the properties been completely depreciated within
the corporation, this would not have been such an onerous
expense. But now, there was no escape: he was forced, in effect,

to pay a double capital gains tax. It cost him $60,000 to transfer ownership from his own corporation to himself as an individual, though not a penny changed hands. He was compelled to sell one-fourth of his assets in order to meet the tax. This procedure seems eminently unfair because when property is transferred to the corporation — or to a trust — its basis constitutes the amount so conveyed.

The lesson from this man's experience is that the owner should have set up separate corporations for the various buildings if he preferred this form of ownership. Had he done so, his capital gains liability would have been less than one-half of what it finally became.

(4)   The Corporation Which Disbursed Profits Under Court Order

One man invested in the stock of a certain corporation which was making substantial profits but disbursing practically no dividends. Since the shares were selling well below equity values, he invested $200,000 in them. In due course, some of the stockholders, through court action, forced a distribution of surplus, under which our investor received $300,000 in return for his original investment. Believing the $100,000 to be capital gain, he paid the 25 per cent tax on this.

In auditing his return, the IRS declared this payout a dividend subject to a tax of up to 70 per cent.

The lesson here is that when the stockholders sued the corporation, they should have insisted on being paid in stock, a transaction which would have been an exchange of like for like and therefore immune to taxation.

(5)   The Case of the Mortgaged Corporation

Two men, one much older than the other, formed a corporation to sell automobiles: each invested $10,000 and received one-half of the stock. They worked hard and paid themselves modest salaries in order to keep down their own income taxes and to permit a rapid growth of corporate assets, which, after a number of years, reached $200,000. The older man then decided to retire and offered to sell his equity for $100,000.

Since no outside buyer could be found and since the partner had no funds to purchase the stock, he mortgaged the corporate property in order to purchase the older man's shares, which thereupon became treasury stock. The remaining partner was now the sole owner of a company which had a debt of $100,000. The retiring partner paid a capital gains tax of $22,500 on his profit of $90,000.

Never dreaming that he could have become involved in an IRS trap, the younger man was literally stunned when informed that he had received a "constructive dividend" of $100,000. Incredible as it may seem, the IR Code provides in Section 544(a)(1) that "Stock owned, directly or indirectly, by or for a corporation . . . shall be considered as being owned proportionately by the shareholders . . ." The surviving partner was assessed a levy of about $60,000. Because of the $100,000 paid the retiring partner, the IRS demanded $82,500 even though the 16th Amendment states that only income may be taxed and that here, instead of income, there was only a new debt.

The results were tragic. The corporation could not borrow more money on its remaining collateral; the owner had none on which he could obtain credit. Since the IRS would not grant an extension and no alternative remained, he lost his business and his home and was forced to go to work as a mechanic. Although he told his story to a congressional committee, nothing has been done to change the situation in which such devastation may recur.

The lesson here is that individuals in similar situations should make a careful study of what might result from such transactions. The man we have been discussing might have purchased his partner's stock on the installment plan; or, in any event, he should have refused to mortgage the corporation assets in order to transform his partner's equity into treasury stock.

(6)   The Man Who Invested in Vacant Lots

Among my friends in Detroit was an astute businessman who purchased more than one thousand building sites during the middle Thirties; these had been sold in the previous decade at prices ranging upward from $1,000 on the slogan that those who

invest in land near a growing metropolis will never become
indigent in their old age. After the Great Depression struck,
however, nearly all of these, even when fully paid for, were
surrendered to the government for unpaid taxes. After WW II,
my friend sold his lots, which cost him about $35,000, at a profit
exceeding $1 million, on which he paid the capital gains tax of
twenty five per cent.

Then the IRS went into action: although the Code does not so
state, the Agency held that his vacant properties were similar to
a store inventory and that he was in the same position as a realtor
or broker — although, in fact, he was neither. Considering this
ruling not only absurd but also contrary both to law and to
reason, he appealed, at a cost of about $200,000, all the way to the
Supreme Court, which upheld the Internal Revenue Service and
which, in turn, levied a tax reaching 91% on his gain, in addition
to interest and penalties totalling nearly $200,000. In short, his
profit of $1,100,000 finally cost him more than $1,300,000, which
brought on his premature death.

The lesson here is that instead of investing in many smaller
parcels of vacant land, he could have put his money in a smaller
number of larger ones, the sales of which would have been
treated as capital transactions. Or he could have invested in
General Motors stock (which had fallen from 83 to 3 between 1929
and 1933) and in other industrials which in time increased in price
comparably with his vacant lots. And again the supreme warning
to investors follows: be absolutely certain of future contingencies
before taking any plunge into an uncertain domain.

B. THE CYCLE OF BLUFF

In thousands of cases where the IRS cannot utilize a real or a
borderline provision to enmesh its victim, it may invent or create
one by misinterpretation in order to accomplish the same
objective. The following are typical cases of bluff, whose name is
legion.

(1) The Case of the Used-Car Dealer

About 1962, a man stumbled, as it were, into the used-car
business. Having repaired an old jalopy, he put it in front of his

home with a "for sale" sign on it; and, after it was sold at a profit, he acquired another and disposed of it in the same manner. He then rented a vacant lot, purchased several old cars, put them in good operating condition, and sold them at prices which produced a rapidly increasing income.

His method was quite unorthodox: he accepted small down payments, carried his own paper, *charged no interest*, and *did not require the purchasers to carry insurance*. Since he was putting competitors out of business and depriving banks and insurance companies of huge profits, he suspected that they put pressure on the IRS to attack him.

His business increased phenomenally; in a few years, his annual sales exceeded $200,000. But, since his capital was tied up in merchandise and in notes receivable and since he repaired his cars himself, he had neither leisure nor a cash surplus.

Then one day an IRS agent strode into his office to conduct a "routine" audit. The dealer felt that he had nothing to fear, since he had made full disclosure and paid all taxes promptly. On the second day, however, the agent declared that his method of keeping books and paying taxes must be changed from cash to accrual, which meant that when a car was sold for $1,000 with a down payment of $200, the entire amount must be reported as immediate income and the full tax paid thereon. On this basis, the agent assessed a deficiency of $39,500; and, even though no fraud had even been hinted, a fifty per cent penalty — applicable only in cases of willful fraud — was added.

The dealer was stunned: he could not believe that this was the law. He therefore began writing to his congressmen and to the President, from whom he received no more response or consideration than if he had written to Santa Claus. When he explained his predicament to a lawyer, he was told that the IRS has the power to order such a change in the method of bookkeeping and paying taxes. He sought a conference at the IRS District Office, where the conferee upheld the agent; he even went to the Appellate — but without a brief — where the same result ensued.

Desperate, he then offered the certificates of title to purchasers of his cars at discounts up to fifty per cent; and thus regained a portion of his investment. Returning to the Appellate officer, he explained that there was now nothing for the IRS to seize and that he was out of business. The IRS then agreed to accept his past returns as filed if he would agree to use the accrual method in the future — an offer which was too little and too late. Thereupon, the ruined man retired to a small farm, where he wrung a precarious living from the soil, like a peasant, meanwhile still living in terror because of what the IRS might do.

In this case, the IRS proceeded on the basis of pure bluff. Ironically, as authority for its action, it cited Sections 453 and 481(a) of the Code, which specifically permit any business to report as taxable income only that portion of payments received from installments which exceed investment: a determination sustained by literally dozens of court decisions. Had this man studied the law and learned the techniques of self-defense, he could have been saved; and would today be an independent and successful businessman.

(2) The Case of the Dissident Publication

A certain magazine which has been issued for many years and which has always been a staunch exponent of limited federal government and free enterprise, has also consistently exposed the machinations of the Federal Reserve System and the Internal Revenue Service.

In 1971, an IRS agent appeared at its office and then spent more than nine days going over every document there. The editor then spent five more at the district office undergoing intensive interrogation. During all this time, no representative of the publication was permitted to present any material or ask any question relating to the purpose or the nature of the investigation or discover what proposals or disallowances the IRS might be contemplating. In due course, however, without giving any reason or explanation, the Agency revoked the 501(c)(4) status of the organization which published the magazine; and assessed a deficiency of $38,500.

A lawyer, who had been entrusted with power-of-attorney, charged $500 for writing a brief note, without even consulting the publishers, in which he agreed to the revocation of exemption.

The publishers than discharged the lawyer and tried to defend themselves as best they could against the vague, unspecified, and unexplained assessments levied against them. At first, they attempted to retain their exempt status, but this was denied by the IRS headquarters in Washington. Years went by, with potential charges for interest and penalties mounting into the stratosphere: but still the IRS failed to release any Bill of Particulars describing the disallowances on which the assessment was based.

There was, in fact, absolutely no basis for revoking the exempt status of the magazine; and even if it had been a corporation-for-profit and had its income been $45,000 greater than it was, there would still have been no tax-liability; for it was operating at a heavy loss and constantly using its prepaid subscriptions to meet current expenses.

Finally, in 1975, the IRS issued its Ninety Day Letter, which meant that the execution of its determination would begin at the expiration of this period unless appeal was made to the Tax Court. However, when this occurred, the publishers filed their appeal and the IRS was finally forced to list its disallowances; whereupon, with the aid of a decent attorney, the government case collapsed.

As the Moment of Truth approached, the IRS admitted that no tax had ever been due; and that it would officially so declare in writing if the editors would agree to the revocation of exempt status. When this compromise was rejected, the IRS finally agreed that the exemption should remain intact.

Thus, after nearly six years of harassment and expenses of nearly $15,000, the IRS admitted that it had been completely wrong throughout.

The lesson to be gleaned from this case is that neither the IRS nor most lawyers are to be trusted. Had the publishers followed the kind of advice that is offered in this book, they would have forced the IRS at the beginning to detail their disallowances in a complete Bill of Particulars. Had that been available, the case could have been settled quickly and with little expense.

(3) The Case of the Continuous Audit

We have met various individuals who have been audited year after year and who, rather than learn how to defend themselves or incur the heavy expense necessary for reliable counsel, have paid annual extortions ranging from a few hundred dollars to more than a thousand. After all, a clever agent can find something on which to hang an assessment in almost any return, especially one which itemizes deductions and allowances; and thus, for two or three hours of his time, he can reap a munificent harvest and be on his way to promotions which may lead to a district directorship.

I recall one victim who had signed quick consent agreements regularly, but who, in desperation, finally called me. When I went over previous returns, I was convinced that improper assessments had been made. Then it was that he decided to do battle on the occasion of the next audit. He followed my suggestion, demanded that the agent reveal the exact nature of his authority for every decision, thus defeated him soundly, paid nothing, and has since been left meticulously alone. It cost him some time and effort, but he soon realized that this was the best investment he had ever made.

(4) The Case of the Testifying Tax-Resister

A medical doctor in a mid-western city who became prominent about 1974-75 as a vocal critic of the IRS and who testified at a hearing held by Senator Montoya's committee in regard to IRS abuses, soon discovered how this Agency can retaliate. In 1975, as a result of an illness, he began drawing disability payments from his own private insurance company. The IRS thereupon ordered the firm either to stop making payments to the doctor or to pay the money to the government, in spite of the fact that such payments are immune to taxation under Section 104 and that no determination had even been made concerning his tax-liability.

It is worthy of note that Senator Montoya of New Mexico, who gave the citizens an opportunity to air their grievances before a congressional committee and who introduced an excellent bill to protect taxpayers from IRS abuses, was defeated for reelection in 1975. After rumors were circulated in the press that he had never been audited in spite of questionable operations, we believe that powerful forces were activated to accomplish his defeat. It is also worthy of note that none of the provisions contained in his S-2342 sponsored by fourteen senators ever became part of the Tax Reform Act of 1976. We therefore conclude that very little can be expected from Congress unless its members become convinced that their lush careers will end forthwith unless they enact a drastic reformation of the tax law.

(5)   The Employee Who Prepared Returns for His Employer

One man who prepared tax returns for his employer was told that he must sign these and include his Social Security number. This, however, is pure bluff, for Sections 6109(a) and 7701(a)(36) of the Code specifically provide that an employee who does such work is not required to sign it or to reveal his SS number.

(6)   Attempts to Obtain Records Illegally

The Tax Reform Act of 1976 has given taxpayers protection which never existed before against attempts by the IRS to obtain records in the hands of third parties; this includes banks, savings and loan associations, CPAs, bookkeepers, lawyers, or whatever. If the IRS wishes to examine the records of any taxpayer in the possession of a third party, it must inform the taxpayer of this desire and give him fourteen days in which to declare that he opposes such examination. The IRS must then, if it wishes to pursue the case further, appeal to a U.S. District Court for an order to permit such examination; however, even if such permission is given, this can be appealed to the United States Circuit Court of Appeals and even to the United States Supreme Court. In the meantime, no records may be examined.

However, we have already been apprised of cases occurring after February 28, 1977, in which the IRS has attempted to gain possession by the old method of issuing a 2039A "vest-pocket" summons or subpoena. When and if this is done, it is based on pure bluff; and if it obtains any information by any method except that authorized in Section 7609 of the Code (which we reproduce in the Appendix), it is guilty of a felony and no information so obtained may be used legally in any proceeding against the taxpayer.

(7) Pressure to Include Social Security Numbers on 1099s

Under IRS regulations, all persons or corporations who pay interest, royalties, dividends, or commercial rentals, or who make certain other types of payments, are expected to prepare Form 1099 in triplicate for each such payment, send one to the IRS, another to the recipient of the money, and retain one for their own files. Pressure has been exerted by the IRS upon all of these, especially banks and savings and loan associations, to include the Social Security number of every payee.

However, research has failed to reveal any authority by which to enforce this requirement, except on Form W-4 and W-2, which are used in connection with Social Security reports. Nowhere does the Code say that a SS number is required elsewhere. In all other cases, therefore, the IRS is bluffing; and when those who pay dividends, interest, royalties, or rentals, etc., try to obtain the SS numbers of recipients on Form 3435 (used to report them) these can be refused with legal impunity.

I have observed many 1099 forms which do not include the SS number. Should your bank or savings and loan association demand it, you should simply ignore the request and see what happens; if you are told that it is required by law, demand that the law be read to you, which cannot be done, since there is no such law. You will probably find that your banker was himself misinformed and that he will be delighted to learn the truth and handle your account without your SS number. Public Law 97-397 and IRS Regulation 103.34 and 103.35 sometimes cited, merely provide for voluntary disclosure of Social Security numbers.

C. THE CYCLE OF MISINTERPRETATION

(1) Concerning the Depreciation of Commercial Property

When the owner of a shopping center, a warehouse, an apartment building, a fourplex, or even a single rental unit makes his return, he can take a certain percentage deduction for

depreciation; if the property is new, he may take a four per cent
rate, which the IRS may try to reduce to three. This has always
been a fertile field for dispute in which it is extremely important
to prevent the use of bluff by the government.

For any new residential property, a depreciation rate fifty
per cent greater than the straight-line may be taken on the
declining balance. However, he will set up separate schedules for
various components: roof, stoves, refrigerators, carpeting,
furniture, air conditioning, etc.

If the property is, let us say, fifteen or twenty years old
when acquired, a composite depreciation schedule approximately
double that of a new structure may properly be claimed by the
straight-line method.

In making these determinations, the owner should never
yield to IRS misinterpretation. If he will present his case
properly, most or at least a large portion of income from
commercial rentals will be immune to income taxation until the
property is fully paid for or depreciated. Statistics published by
the IRS show that the revenues from nearly one-half of all rental
properties are normally exempt from taxation; in short, such
investments, when properly made and managed, constitute one of
the most desirable tax-shelters anywhere available.

(2)   Concerning the Office in the Home

The Tax Reform Act of 1976 placed certain restrictions on
deductions available to taxpayers for use of office space in their
homes; however, deductions may still be taken for this reason
provided the employer does not furnish facilities for the same
use. In other words, no consideration is now given to those who,
like teachers and various office workers, do a portion only of their
work at home.

But anyone who operates entirely out of his own home and
earns income from work done there still qualifies for a deduction.
Dentists, lawyers, doctors, authors, cartoonists, architects, etc.,
whose offices are in their homes are entitled to deductions equal
to the rental value of whatever portion of such domicile is used as
an office, for storage, or other needs pertinent to their
occupations.

The IRS may attempt to reduce such allowances in the case of an unencumbered home to the proportional cost of utilities, taxes, and similar outlays. However, the taxpayer should never succumb to such misinterpretation: he is entitled to deduct the full rental value of the space used in his occupation. If utilities total $1,500 in a house which would rent for $4,500; and if one-fifth of the area is used occupationally, the taxpayer is entitled to deduct at least $1,200. And this should not be reported as an itemized deduction, but as an integral portion of business expenses.

The only restriction is that total income from the occupation must be at least equal to the claimed deduction.

(3) Reimbursement for Travel Expenses While on Business

The IRS may tell an individual who receives reimbursement for personal expenses incurred while travelling either for an employer paying a salary or some other entity making reimbursements that he can report as a deduction only his actual, itemized costs. This is not true unless his expenses exceed $44 a day in 1977-78 ($25.00 for a room and $19.00 for meals and incidentals). In other words, if he is very economical and spends considerably less, he can still receive this sum for daily expenses *without itemizing any current tax-deductions.* Such amounts will certainly increase with inflation.

If the total compensation covers travel expenses only and does not involve or include any salary or honorarium, we do not consider it necessary to report the reimbursement at all.

(4) Concerning the Perjury Line

I have an extensive file of correspondence with officials of the IRS dealing with the perjury line in which they declare that if a taxpayer deletes this on his 1040, this return is regarded as none at all; that in such case, the statute of limitations will never begin to run; and that the taxpayer can be prosecuted criminally under Section 7203 for failure to file, *even though he has made complete and accurate disclosure and has paid all taxes due.* The reason for this is, of course, that when this line is deleted, the government loses the power to prosecute criminally for fraud and can only undertake a civil action.

However, it has come to my attention that various individuals whose returns are otherwise "proper" and complete have blotted out the perjury line without any challenge from the IRS. Were this to occur, it would have to be a criminal prosecution for failure to file; and it would indeed be interesting to see whether a taxpayer would be sent to prison by a jury where the accused had made complete disclosure and paid all taxes, merely for deleting the perjury line. Since neither fraud nor underpayment of taxes could be alleged, would any jury convict in a prosecution of this nature? On the other hand, should the Supreme Court refuse to find a taxpayer guilty of a crime for erasing the perjury line, all IRS power to prosecute criminally could be terminated. In short, here again the IRS operates on the basis of legal misinterpretation; and if this were removed, its administration would become virtually impossible.

D. THE CYCLE OF UNCONSTITUTIONAL PROCEDURES

(a) The Seizure of the Taxpayer's Property

The Fifth Amendment in our Bill of Rights declares that no one shall be deprived of Life, Liberty, or PROPERTY without due process of law. Whenever, therefore, the IRS seizes an automobile or other personal property, including a bank account, or occupies or places a lien on real estate without observing the requirements of due process, it commits a violation of the Constitution. Since the IRS has been guilty in this respect millions of times, it emerges as perhaps the greatest known lawbreaker. United States District Court judges, the members of the Supreme Court, and our senators and representatives in the Congress, must be aware of this: and yet they all become stone deaf when anyone attempts to bring these facts to their attention. No congressional committee, to my knowledge, has ever permitted any testimony on this sensitive subject; and no bill has ever reached the floor of Congress which would compel the IRS to obey the Constitution. We find, therefore, that the Congress places unconstitutional provisions in the IR Code and that the courts then enforce them, no matter how blatantly they violate our Bill of Rights, which was erected specifically to prevent in this nation any recurrence of the tyrannies from which our Founding Fathers had suffered so bitterly.

(2)   The Seizure of Property Owned by Third Parties

However, the IRS is not satisfied by committing acts which merely violate the Constitution: nor does it limit its felonies to such acts as opening first-class mail, burglarizing homes and offices, tapping telephones, offering perjured testimony in court, etc.; it also constantly tramples on its own law thousands of times every year by seizing and occupying property which it is specifically forbidden to touch. Section 6331(b) of its Code states that "The term 'levy' as used in this title includes the power of distraint and seizure by any means." If words have meaning, this implies that IRS agents may use kidnapping, terror, murder, and any other method with impunity in order to accomplish the distraint and seizure of property. However, the same provision then declares: "A levy shall extend only to property possessed and obligations existing at the time thereof" (i.e., the seizure). This means that no levy or distraint may be placed upon any property except that belonging to the delinquent taxpayer or on obligations due from a third party to him. The IRS is therefore categorically forbidden to seize any real estate belonging to a third party who is not involved in a specific dispute and does not owe anything to the person who is so involved.

However, the IRS routinely violates this provision of its own law. When any person occupying a rental office, warehouse, store, or other building has a dispute with the Service, it normally seizes the premises, changes the locks, posts it as government property, and makes the direst threats against owners who might dare to enter their premises without government permission. Thus, thousands of property owners have been astounded to discover that their own buildings have become government property without notice to them.

The IRS, of course, finds it convenient to use the landlord's premises to store the personal property of a delinquent while he is given a certain period to produce payment or have his

possessions sold at auction — for little or nothing. Actually, the
IRS has no more authority to seize such real estate in this manner
than it would have to enter some other building, throw the owner
or tenant into the street, use the structure to store the seized
personal property, and, in due course, conduct an auction on that
site.

Even though the IRS has probably committed this felony
millions of times, I do not know of any successful challenge to
such action, except that some property owners, by taking
the IRS to court, have been able to collect the bare rent from
them, but only for the exact number of days during which the
property was posted as government premises and then only if the
owner could prove that he had received no rental from the tenant
for this period.

(3)   Compelling Testimony from a Taxpayer

The Fifth Amendment states that no citizen in a criminal
case shall be compelled to give testimony against himself. The
manner in which the IRS attempts to evade this constitutional
provision is wonderful to contemplate.

In the first place, Section 6012 of the Code provides that all
persons receiving certain incomes shall make a return; section
7203 then provides that in case Section 6012 applies, the
punishment for failing to file may be one year in prison and a fine
of $10,000, or both, on each count. Section 6065(a) then adds that
every return must be made under penalties of perjury; and
finally Sections 6531, 6653(b), 6674, and 7201-17, spell out in detail
the penalties which may be imposed for any misstatement in, or
omission from, a tax return.

So the basic law (6012) does not require that a tax be paid;
but later we find that a return must be made; and then that it must
be made under penalties of perjury and in a form which discloses
income and admits tax-liability.

Thus, Section 7203 does not inflict punishment for fraud or
non-payment of taxes; but only for failure to file.

If ever there was a jesuitical document, it is the Internal
Revenue Code. You are not forced to make disclosure of income,
but if you do not file, you are subject to fine and imprisonment

for neglecting to do so. You are not forced to pay a tax as such, but if you do not make disclosure, you are guilty of a misde-meanor; and if you are guilty of a misstatement or an omission, you commit a felony punishable by three years in prison, since your return must be made under penalties of perjury.

The fact is that by this roundabout method, the government forces you to give evidence against yourself; it maintains that it does not violate the Fifth Amendment because the evidence it seeks is civilian in nature and presumed to be honest. And since, according to the courts, this is given voluntarily, it involves the waiving of all Fifth Amendment rights even if it is fraudulent. But if you give no evidence "voluntarily," you can be fined $10,000 and sent to prison. Is that not compelled testimony?

We can see no way by which the government can escape the charge that the IRS forces citizens to give evidence which can incriminate them; in fact, nearly all IRS prosecutions result from information in some way related to the 1040 form already submitted under duress.

Every such return, to be legal under our Bill of Rights, should carry the Miranda Warning printed in red letters at the top. And the protections granted those whose incomes derive from illegal sources under *Marchetti, Grosso,* and *Garner v. the United States* should be extended to every taxpayer: namely the right to refuse to give any information at all. We wonder why criminals should have privileges which honest taxpayers do not!

Actually, no individual should be forced to give the govern-ment the kind of information demanded on the 1040 form. If this requirement did not exist in the IR Code, it would be mandatory for the government to determine each person's income, and bill him on the basis of its own computation; incidentally, this method would be comparable to that on which property assessments are made and taxes collected. We consider any other method definitely unconstitutional.

(4)   Deficiencies for Refusing an Examination of Records

There is another field in which the IRS violates not only the Fourth and Fifth Amendments, but also Supreme Court decisions, notably the landmark opinion issued in *Boyd v. United*

States, decided on February 1, 1886.

Whenever an IRS agent comes to your office, the first thing he is likely to demand is the right to examine cancelled checks, invoices, receipts, etc., in order to verify your deductions or business expenses. However, since you have already filed your return under penalties of perjury, any implication that you are guilty of omissions or misstatements constitutes a charge of fraud; and, since this is a criminal offense, the burden of proof must be on the government. In other words, it is now demanding not only that you prove your innocence, but also that you give evidence against yourself — if you are not innocent — in a criminal case. In this demand, the government violates the Fourth Amendment which declares that every citizen shall be safe in his papers and effects against unreasonable search and seizure; and it violates the Fifth by requiring the citizen to supply information in what can become a criminal case.

Until several crucial court decisions took this power away from the IRS, it made a practice of sending taxpayers to prison under Section 7203 simply for refusing to answer questions or surrendering personal records: and even though these portions of 7203 are now nugatory, they are still printed in the Code. The IRS cannot, therefore, now threaten prison or confiscation for a refusal to permit an examination of records; but it still possesses a fearful weapon: for in the event of such refusal, it normally and simply disallows all deductions, exemptions, allowances, etc., and recomputes the tax on this basis. The IRS will then give the taxpayer the choice of paying the levy or appealing the determination through the available administrative channels, which are explained in later chapters of this book.

However, when the IRS reassesses a tax-liability in this manner, it is in direct violation of *Boyd*. For in that decision, the Supreme Court declared explicitly that the government cannot use records it obtains under duress of any kind, to recompute the tax either on the basis of the information thus obtained or because it is not surrendered. Thus, whenever the IRS recomputes a tax liability because the taxpayer declines to permit an examination of his records, it violates the Constitution and disregards the explicit declarations of the Supreme Court.

We think that every taxpayer facing an audit should use
Boyd (of which we reproduce the most important portions in the
Appendix) to the hilt, and ask the agent whether he believes in
the Constitution or in Supreme Court decisions. If he cites other
decisions which run counter to *Boyd*, the taxpayer might declare
that since the Supreme Court evidently does not know what the
law is, we should go back to, and abide by, the plain words of the
Constitution.

It would be interesting indeed to have a tape containing the
answers of an IRS agent to such questions.

(5)   *The Refusal to Grant Jury Trials*

The Seventh Amendment in our Bill of Rights declares that
"in suits at common law, where the value in controversy shall
exceed twenty dollars, the right of trial by jury shall be
preserved . . ." Since the Common Law is the civil law, this should
apply to all disputes between citizens and the IRS. Whenever,
therefore, such a dispute involves more than twenty dollars, the
citizen has a constitutional right to a jury trial.

However, there is no jury trial in the Internal Revenue
Service or even in the Tax Court even if the dispute involves
millions of dollars. There is only one way that a citizen can obtain
such an adjudication under the IR Code; and that is by first
paying every penny demanded and then suing for a refund in a
United States District Court, where the burden of proof will rest
entirely upon the aggrieved and perhaps already bankrupt
taxpayer, who will receive no reimbursement for his expenses,
even if he wins the suit.

(6)   *The Jeopardy Assessment*

One of the most cruel, oppressive, and unconstitutional of all
the acts perpetrated by the IRS has been the Jeopardy
Assessment, authorized under Sections 6851, 6861, and 6862,
especially when invoked without need or when no actual tax-
liability had been determined. The pretext for this was that
unless the IRS could seize all assets without notice, these might
be concealed or removed to a foreign country. However, this was
not the way it operated; for whenever the Service decided to

destroy an individual, it seized everything he owned without warning. The Nevada multi-millionaire uranium king, Charles Steen, thus found himself penniless and was able to survive only through the charity of friends. Howard McCanse of Oregon, after several years of misery, was able to prove the IRS dead wrong on every count, but at a cost of $500,000 to himself. When the Honorable J. Bracken Lee, governor of Utah, placed a portion of his tax in 1954 in escrow until the courts should adjudicate the constitutionality of foreign giveaways, all of his assets were frozen until he released the disputed tax to the IRS.

After invoking this dreadful authority, it was the practice of the Agency to issue a Letter of Deficiency which usually demanded a payment many times greater than could possibly be due; and while the victim, being without funds, could not meet his obligations, he became bankrupt and the IRS sold his assets for little or nothing. Then, since only a small portion of the alleged deficiency was realized, the pauperized taxpayer remained subject to endless, successive seizures of anything he might acquire in the future.

This outrageous situation, however, has been partially corrected in the Tax Reform Act of 1976, which provides in Section 7429 that the IRS must, within five days of seizure, give the taxpayer a written statement of the information upon which its assessment is based; that the taxpayer may, within thirty days, request a review of such statement and a final determination by the Agency; that he may have an extension of twenty or even sixty days before execution; that the burden of proof shall be upon the IRS; and that no confiscation may proceed while a determination is pending in a United States District Court.

E. SUMMARY

Jefferson once said that the time might come when human beings would hire themselves out to the government to fasten their own chains upon their fellow-sufferers; and if this applies fully to any group today, it must be the agents of the Internal

Revenue Service. To me, it is incredible that decent men and women would engage in such activities merely to make a living; I would have more respect for them if they were bank-robbers or second-story thieves. It seems to me that I would infinitely prefer to starve than carry out the duties which I have often seen them perform. On the other hand, I know that many individuals are so constituted that they find an intense emotional pleasure and satisfaction from inflicting torture upon others or in a sense of personal domination. Of course, it may be that some agents have actually persuaded themselves that they are engaged in a patriotic duty, which consists in preventing evaders from escaping their fair share of taxation. Whatever the motives of agents may be, it is certain that their positions confer upon them a power which their own talents could never procure for them in the open market. It seems to me that many IRS agents are willing to work for a median compensation so that they can exercise power over fellow creatures, who are often reduced to begging for mercy, even where there is no mercy: for, according to one former IRS official, every agent takes an oath that he will never be influenced by any feeling of sympathy which he might develop for a suffering taxpayer, facing impoverishment or economic destruction, because of IRS harassment and assessments.

Four — Techniques of Tax Reduction and Avoidance

A. THE W-4 FORM

Wage-workers as well as salaried personnel have at their disposal various methods by which to protect their paychecks. Millions have already learned how to do this and more millions could be doing so soon. Since all methods suggested here are entirely legal, they may be practiced without fear of reprisal.

Employees of whatever status normally submit to their employers the W-4 Form — the Employees Withholding Allowance Certificate — which, by stating the number of exemptions and deductions which are claimed, determines the portion of pay which is exempt from withholding. Nothing could please the employer more than to place the entire pay of his employees in their envelopes.

Until 1972, the W-4 Form was simply a statement of exemptions. Since many other deductions could be taken on final returns by itemizing, there was generally heavy overwithholding and employees filed their 1040s in order to obtain substantial refunds which usually totalled tens of billions of dollars.

The current W-4 Form, which became effective Dec. 31, 1978, is reproduced on the following page. The upper portion of this, which is to be filed with the employer, states the number of allowances claimed. Each of these reduces taxable income by $1,000, and includes all exemptions as well as other deductions to which the employee is entitled, such as payments for interest, taxes, casualties, medical expenses, contributions to religion or

Form W-4
(Rev. December 1978)
Department of the Treasury
Internal Revenue Service

Employee's Withholding Allowance Certificate
(Use for Wages Paid After December 31, 1978)
This certificate is for income tax withholding purposes only. It will remain in effect until you change it. If you claim exemption from withholding, you will have to file a new certificate on or before April 30 of next year.

Type or print your full name
John W. Taxpayer

Your social security number
000-00-0000

Home address (number and street or rural route)
0000 City Street

City or town, State, and ZIP code
Anytown, State 00000

Marital Status
☐ Single ☒ Married
☐ Married, but withhold at higher Single rate
Note: If married, but legally separated, or spouse is a nonresident alien, check the single block.

1 Total number of allowances you are claiming 23
2 Additional amount, if any, you want deducted from each pay (if your employer agrees) . . . . $
3 I claim exemption from withholding (see instructions). Enter "Exempt" . . . .

Under the penalties of perjury, I certify that the number of withholding allowances claimed on this certificate does not exceed the number to which I am entitled. If claiming exemption from withholding, I certify that I incurred no liability for Federal income tax for last year and I anticipate that I will incur no liability for Federal income tax for this year.

Signature ▶ .... Date ▶ ...., 19..........

.... Detach along this line ....

▲ Give the top part of this form to your employer; keep the lower part for your records and information ▲

Instructions

The explanatory material below will help you determine your correct number of withholding allowances, and will assist you in completing the Form W-4 at the top of this page.

See Publication 505 for more information on withholding.

Avoid Overwithholding or Underwithholding

By claiming the number of withholding allowances you are entitled to, you can fit the amount of tax withheld from your wages to your tax liability. In addition to the allowances for personal exemptions to be claimed in item (a), be sure to claim any additional allowances you are entitled to in item (b), "Special withholding allowance," and item (c), "Allowance(s) for credit(s) and/or deduction(s)." While you may claim these allowances on Form W-4 for withholding purposes, you may not claim them under "Exemptions" on your tax return Form 1040 or Form 1040A.

You may claim the special withholding allowance if you are single with only one employer, or married with only one employer and your spouse is not employed. If you have unusually large itemized deductions, make alimony payments, or credit(s) for child care expenses, earned income, credit for the elderly, or residential energy credits, you may claim additional allowances to avoid having too much income tax withheld from your wages.

If you and your spouse are both employed or you have more than one employer, you should make sure that enough has been withheld. If you find that you need more withholding, claim fewer allowances or ask for additional withholding or request to be withheld at the higher "Single" status. If you are currently claiming additional withholding allowances based on

itemized deductions, check the worksheet on the back to see that you are claiming the proper number of allowances.

How Many Withholding Allowances May You Claim?

Use the schedule below to determine the number of allowances you may claim for tax withholding purposes. In determining the number, keep in mind these points: if you are single and hold more than one job, you may not claim the same allowances with more than one employer at the same time; or, if you are married and both you and your spouse are employed, you may not both claim the same allowances with your employers at the same time. A nonresident alien, other than a resident of Canada, Mexico, or Puerto Rico, may claim only one personal allowance.

Completing Form W-4

If you find you are entitled to one or more allowances in addition to those you are now claiming, increase your number of allowances by completing the form above and filing it with your employer. If the number of allowances you previously claimed decreases, you must file a new Form W-4 within 10 days. (If you expect to owe more tax than will be withheld, you may increase your withholding by claiming fewer or "0" allowances on line 1, or by asking for additional withholding on line 2, or both.)

You may claim exemption from withholding of Federal income tax if you had no liability for income tax for last year, and you anticipate that you will incur no liability for income tax for this year. You may not claim exemption if your joint or separate return shows tax liability before the allowance of any credit for income tax withheld. If you are exempt, your employer will not withhold Federal income tax from your wages. However, social security tax

will be withheld if you are covered by the Federal Insurance Contributions Act.

You must revoke this exemption (1) within 10 days from the time you anticipate you will incur income tax liability for the year or (2) on or before December 1 if you anticipate you will incur Federal income tax liability for the next year. If you want to stop or are required to revoke this exemption, you must file a new Form W-4 with your employer showing the number of withholding allowances you are entitled to claim. This certificate for exemption from withholding will expire on April 30 of next year unless a new Form W-4 is filed on or before that date.

The Following Information is Provided in Accordance with the Privacy Act of 1974

The Internal Revenue Code requires every employee to furnish his or her employer with a signed withholding allowance certificate showing the number of withholding allowances that the employee claims (section 3402(f)(2)(A) and the Regulations thereto). Individuals are required to provide their Social Security Number for proper identification and processing (section 6109 and the Regulations thereto).

The principal purpose for soliciting withholding allowance certificate information is to administer the Internal Revenue laws of the United States.

If an employee does not furnish a signed withholding allowance certificate, the employee is considered as claiming no withholding allowances (section 3401(e)) and shall be treated as a single person (section 3402(l)).

The routine uses of the withholding allowance certificate information include disclosure to the Department of Justice for actual or potential criminal prosecution or civil litigation.

Figure Your Total Withholding Allowances Below

(a) Allowance(s) for exemption(s)—Enter 1 for each personal exemption you can claim on your Federal income tax return* . . . 8
(b) Special withholding allowance—Enter 1 if single with 1 employer, or married with 1 employer and spouse not employed** . . . 1
(c) Allowance(s) for credit(s) and/or deduction(s)—Enter number from tables on page 2 14
(d) Total (add lines (a) through (c) above)—Enter here and on line 1, Form W-4, above 23

*If you are in doubt as to whom you may claim as a dependent, see the instructions that came with your last Federal income tax return or call your local Internal Revenue Service office.
**This allowance is used solely for purposes of figuring your withholding tax, and cannot be claimed when you file your tax return.

charity, etc. Dependent children can earn up to $2,300 tax-free
and still qualify as exemptions for parents or guardians; or they
can earn $3,300 without being required to file a return. If a man
and wife under 65 are without dependants, they are entitled to an
automatic exemption of $3,400 plus $1,000 plus $2,000, which
entitle them to seven allowances. If they are over 65, they are
automatically exempt from tax on two more allowances. If both
are blind, they are entitled to two more. If a couple has ten
dependants, the automatic exemption is $14,400, or fifteen
allowances. If this income consists of wages or a salary subject to
withholding, the taxpayer is not required to file the 1040 at all,
and will do so only in case he is entitled to a refund.

   Perhaps the best part of the W-4 Form is the provision for an
additional allowance for each expected itemized deduction or
fraction thereof, to be reported on the 1040. If a person pays
other taxes — real estate, personal property, state income, etc.
— totalling $3,000, he has three allowances for these. If he pays
interest on mortgages, credit-card balances, installment sales,
contract purchases, etc., totalling $2,000, he has two more. If he
makes contributions of $2,000 to religious or charitable organiza-
tions, he will have two allowances for these. If he has medical
expenses of $2,000 above the threshold deduction, he has two
more allowances; if he has a hospital bill, not covered by
insurance, of $3,000, this will provide three. If he suffered a
casualty or loss of any kind, such as fire, theft, accident, or
misplacement, this could easily account for several additional
allowances. If he has a bad-debt or investment loss, this could
create several more legal allowances.

   The W-4 Form on page 39 reflects the situation of a man
with a non-working wife, 6 dependants, and 14 itemized
allowances, making a total of 23, under which $23,000 of income
will be exempt from withholding — which would be $433 a week
or nearly $2,000 a month.

   We suggest that the number of allowances claimed be based
upon practical expectations. All likely deductions should be
included, for life is filled with uncertainties, exigencies, and
accidents; and should there be two or three more than may
eventuate, no harm need be done, since any tax due can be paid

in the following April. Surely there is no reason why anyone should permit the government to hold a taxpayer's money without paying interest thereon.

Some employees have reported a very large number of allowances, such as 99, which could be correct because of large contributions to charity and heavy casualty or investment losses. Since it is to the advantage of the taxpayer that withholding be reduced at least to the level of actual taxation, we suggest that all reasonable allowances be reported.

As we have already shown, a man with a wife and five children is not required to make a return on wages until this compensation exceeds $11,400; if there are ten dependants, this immunity rises to $16,400.

Note that the W-4 Form consists of two parts: the lower portion thereof should be filled out and retained by the employee for his own information; the upper portion will be completed and filed with the employer, who will automatically adjust his withholding in accordance with it.

Every employee who has not already filed the most advantageous W-4 Form possible, should do so without delay.

One of the principal reasons why returns are audited for verification is a suspicion that deductions are inflated or fraudulent. However, the IRS is not likely to question them unless they exceed substantially the national norm, which we reproduce in the table on page 42 taken from the 1979 *Master Tax Guide*, page 391. These ratios have been rising annually.

B.   *THE EXEMPT LINE ON FORM W-4*

If no tax was due or paid during the preceding year, and if none is expected to be due during the present, the employee may legally write *Exempt* on Line 3 of the W-4 Form and file it with his employer. The Instructions state that

> You may claim exemption from withholding of Federal Income tax if you had no liability for income tax for last year, and you anticipate that you will incur no liability for income tax for this year ... If you are exempt, your employer will not withhold Federal income tax from your wages...

You must revoke this exemption (1) within 10 days from the time you anticipate you will incur federal income tax liability for the year of (2) on or before December 1 if you anticipate you will incur Federal income tax liability for the next year. If you want to stop or are required to revoke this exemption, you must file a new Form W-4 with your employer showing the number of withholding allowances you are entitled to claim.

This provision was added primarily for seasonal workers such as students, who ordinarily would not earn more than $2,300. However, there are millions of others who, having had a sufficient number of exemptions and/or other allowances to eliminate federal income taxation in one year, are eligible to file for total exemption. In any event, the moment this is done, it becomes mandatory for the employer to cease all income-tax withholding, and he does not need to report such cessation until

AVERAGE ITEMIZED DEDUCTIONS FOR 1976 BY ADJUSTED GROSS INCOME CLASSES

Adjusted Gross Income Classes	Average Deductions for Contributions	Average Deductions for Interest	Average Deductions for Taxes	Average Medical Expense Deductions	Deductions As Portion of Total Income	As Per-cent of Total Income
$ 5,000-$ 6,000	$ 428	$1,106	$ 776	$ 845	$3,155	60%
6,000- 7,000	392	1,180	918	862	3,352	49%
7,000- 8,000	453	1,056	870	1,170	3,549	45%
8,000- 9,000	393	1,193	903	906	3,395	39%
9,000- 10,000	441	1,268	958	896	3,563	37%
10,000- 15,000	414	1,378	1,129	655	3,576	28%
15,000- 20,000	472	1,690	1,503	585	4,251	25%
20,000- 25,000	542	1,836	1,869	487	4,734	22%
25,000- 30,000	646	1,977	2,262	442	5,327	20%
30,000- 50,000	939	2,366	3,050	523	6,878	19%
50,000- 100,000	2,015	3,954	5,383	700	12,052	19%
100,000-or more	9,901	9,249	13,274	1,095	33,519	20%

the close of his fiscal year. Every one should be warned, however, that if he has admitted taxable income during the previous year, he is not eligible to write Exempt on Line 3 of the W-4 Form.

The IRS is more sensitive to claims for total exemption than it is to a reasonable overestimation of allowances. If the Service decides to prosecute, it must do so on a felony charge, which is difficult to prove and requires a jury trial.

In 1975, there were 20,424,000 returns which paid no income taxes; and it is certain that in addition to millions which were exempt because of low incomes there were many others who, by giving generously to charity, setting up their own churches or trusts, or utilizing other valid techniques, legally avoided taxation on substantial incomes. If they received wages or salaries not exceeding the amounts set forth in the Introduction of this work, they were entitled to file exempt W-4 Forms; and by utilizing exemptions, allowances, exclusions, and other deductions permitted by the Code many more will be able to achieve the position of the New York banker mentioned in a previous chapter. We find that for fiscal 1969, there were 1,211 returns with reported Adjusted Gross Income exceeding $1 million: of these, 52 paid no tax whatever, and a great many others paid only a small percentage. Of 82,211 with incomes exceeding $100,000, there were 845 which were totally exempt from federal income taxation.[A] And when we realize that these returns were from people who collected most of the $20 or $25 billion of revenue generated by exempt securities in 1974-75 — as well as many other forms of non-reportable income — we begin to comprehend their enormous extent. We should note that those whose incomes consist of non-reportable categories are not required to file any return at all, a fact which would increase the number of super-wealthy listed as paying no tax well above the totals revealed in the statistics.

C. GOING ON CONTRACT

There is another and simple means available in the employee-employer relationship which is being utilized to an ever-increasing extent: *going on contract* — using a form like the one reproduced on the next page, a step which transforms the employee into an independent sub-contractor and which places him in the category of the self-employed, like ministers or proprietors.

It is only necessary that the employer and employee agree upon the terms of compensation, conditions of work, the nature and amount of performance, etc., just as any sub-contractor does with the general contractor on a construction project or as any entrepreneur — such as a painter or carpenter — does when he agrees to perform a certain job for a home-owner at an agreed-upon price.

Imagine the employer's delight with such a relationship! He is relieved of bookkeeping and the duty of transmitting employees' funds to the government as well as the necessity of making Social Security contributions equal to those of his employee and transmitting these also to the central government. The importance of this is emphasized by the growing inflation and the fact that the employer's possible share of an employee's Social Security payments is scheduled to exceed $3,000.00 in 1985. Furthermore, the employer will no longer make any contribution to state unemployment and other programs, which constitute a very heavy drain on his resources.

Under such a contract, each party has a right to terminate the arrangement at will, unless otherwise specified. If the employee has an office of his own, keeps his own books and records, uses his own tools or equipment as far as possible, and offers his services to more than one employer (or at least qualifies under any three of the above) the IRS cannot invalidate his self-employed status. Since the cost of performance will be sharply reduced to the employer, he will gladly fatten the emoluments of such sub-contractor, who will give more in return therefor. Since all concerned will benefit, a sound basis for continued cooperation will be created.

Employers can lump together some of these payments and need not identify all contractees by name, to whom the advantages are perhaps even greater than to the employer. No longer subject to union membership, jurisdiction, or contributions, they can escape the various plans and systems

AGREEMENT AND CONTRACT

KNOW ALL MEN BY THESE PRESENTS:

That this Contract made by and between_____,
Party of the first part, and_____, Address;
_____Party of the Second Part, for the
purpose of establishing an independent Contract relationship and
Contractual Agreement between the parties hereto absolutely ex-
cluding any employee-employer style relationship.
That the party of the First Part and the Party of the Second
Part do covenant and agree as follows:
1. That the Party of the Second Part will provide the following
Kinds of Services:_____

_____

2. That the Party of the Second part will be compensated as
follows: $ _____per hour or_____
payable in cash or Federal Reserve Notes, at the option of the First
Party.
3. All equipment, tools or supplies will be provided by the
Second Party (Possibly employer can pay employee enough that employee
can pay employer rent on the equipment and tools provided by employer.), except as follows:_____

_____

4. The Party of the Second part states and affirms that he is
acting as a free agent and independent Contractor, holding himself
out to the General Public as an Independent Contractor for other
work or Contracts as he sees fit; that he runs adds in the newspapers offering services to the General Public, maintains his office
and principle place of business at his address above stated and
carries business cards; that this Contract is not exclusive. First
Party possesses no Right hereunder to discourage or inhibit the
Second Party's rights to enter any other contracts as he sees fit.
5. This Contract shall run from day to day or until the project
Second Party is hired for is completed, thereby making it impossible
for First Party to fire Second Party; both parties are equally
bound to this Contract; Second Parties pay may be received at any
time upon reasonable demand for work or performance of the Contract
up to the time of the demand; all of the amounts shall be paid in
full with no deductions of any kind.
6. Second party may start work or cease work at will, as long
as the Contract is performed and accomplished satisfactorily and
promptly; no supervision of Second Party will be made by First
Party in the details of the work to be performed after the initial
period of introduction to the object of the Contract described herein.
7. Second party agrees to accept full responsibility for any and
all taxes that may be lawfully due to any governmental unit and to
hold Party of the First Part harmless from any liability from the non-
payment of taxes due from Second Party to any Governmental Unit.
In Witness Whereof, the parties hereto set their hands and Seals
this____day of_____197_.

Witness_____   _____
                               First Party

Witness_____   _____
                               Second Party

under which forty per cent of a worker's compensation is sometimes filched away. Under the contractual system, PAY and TAKE-HOME PAY become identical.

Social Security and income taxes will, of course, be required from the sub-contractors, just as they are from doctors, merchants, motel proprietors, entrepreneurs, and other self-employed individuals. Whatever they contribute to Social Security, however, will be far less than the combined contributions of employers and employees. Furthermore, as self-employed individuals, they will be eligible to invest fifteen per cent or up to $7,500 of tax-free income in their own personal retirement trusts.

D. BECOMING A CHURCH

For a few dollars, the Universal Life Church, founded by Kirby Hensley with headquarters in Modesto, California, has been ordaining any adult a minister, bishop, or even a cardinal. For a small additional fee, it has supplied the new cleric with a complete set of instructions explaining how to file articles of incorporation in his own state, prepare a set of bylaws, establish his church, and carry on his financial affairs. In 1978, this Church had already ordained six million and chartered more than 35,000 churches as branches of its denomination.

Jerome Daly in Minnesota with the Basic Bible Church of America and William Drexler with the Life Science Church in California both offer ministerial ordinations and membership in orders based on the vow of poverty, which purport to offer immunity to all income taxation.

Since a church is a corporate entity established under state authority, it assumes a legally independent existence. Its funds must not be intermingled with those of any individual; it must have a treasury and a bank account of its own.

Although we may expect the old-line churches, fearing the loss of their own preferences, to oppose any extension of their immunities and privileges to such "illegitimate" organizations; and even though the Internal Revenue Service will probably do all in its power to prevent the proliferation of the movement, it is certain that neither the government nor anyone else can prescribe any specific requirement for the establishment of a church so long as it meets certain legal qualifications. With the cooperation of two others, any ordained individual can establish a religious corporation in his own state, draw up a set of bylaws giving himself complete and perpetual control, and, under Section 170(c) of the Code, pay half of his non-church income to the corporation as a deductible contribution. He can deed his home to the Church, take a possible six-year tax-deduction for the gift, which thus becomes a combination sanctuary and parsonage, probably immune to real-estate taxation. Or he can *sell* his home to his church corporation and be repaid over a period of years in non-taxable installments, since these will simply be the repayment of a debt. Every minister is entitled under Section 107 of the IR Code to what is known as a housing allowance, which can cover all expenses necessary for the minister and his family to operate their home, with the exception of food. If he occupies a mortgaged home or one purchased on contract, even the principal payments are deductible. Services can then be held there on a regular basis, in which he may discuss ethics, the Federal Reserve System, the monetary problem, the international situation, the inequities of the Internal Revenue Code and System, states' rights versus federal aggrandizement, etc. The church pays for the operation of the sanctuary-parsonage, including all outlays involved in its maintenance, as well as the minister's travelling and incidental expenses. It can also pay him a salary of several thousand dollars which may be exempt from income taxation. Under Section 1402(c)(4) and (3)(1) and (2) of the Code, any ordained minister may obtain exemption from Social Security contributions on any income received from his church simply by filing Form 4361 with the IRS during the first three years of his pastorate as a conscientious objector to the Social Security retirement plan. In short, the new minister can easily enjoy an income of $20,000 or more a year without the payment of any real estate, income, or Social Security taxes. Or, if he belongs to an established order, he may take the vow of poverty — like a Jesuit — and all his income becomes exempt, since this is turned over to the church, which then supplies all his needs without the necessity of filing any tax returns at all, no matter what standard of living he may be enjoying.

An additional immunity which all churches enjoy is that whereas most other 501(c)(3) organizations must be approved by the IRS before receiving exemption from federal taxation or supervision, such immunity is automatic in the case of any church as soon as it files articles of incorporation with state authorities. Furthermore, whereas other non-profit and tax-exempt entities must file informational returns with the IRS, this does not apply to churches and other religious corporations, which are exempted under Section 508(c) of the Code. Furthermore, under Section 7605, the IRS is prohibited from auditing the books of any church *even if it is in violation of some Internal Revenue law.*

It is possible that millions of Americans may organize their own churches and thus become recipients of the extraordinary advantages and immunities conferred upon such entities in the Internal Revenue Code. If this were done, it could be one of the most important steps that could be taken to terminate forever the IRS and its entire operation.

E. AVOIDING PROBATE: THE INTER VIVOS TRUST

The irrevocable *inter vivos* trust can be utilized by median or substantial middle-class estates to reduce current taxation substantially and to avoid the expense and the delays of probate, the enormous cost of inheritance and estate taxes, and the heavy charges imposed by executors, appraisers, lawyers, and probate courts. Even worse is the case of property left intestate, which will often be eaten up by strangers before any disposition can be made of it; and even that transferred by will may be tied up for years and much of it likewise appropriated. As estates go through probate, it is not unusual for more than twenty or even thirty per cent of them to disappear during several years of delay; and often those of $20,000 to $30,000 leave nothing for designated heirs.

Neither lawyers nor banks are likely to suggest an *inter vivos* (i.e., a living) trust to be established and administered by the owner of real estate or other assets; however, any person can create and manage his own revocable trust as the trustee thereof and dispose of it in whatever manner he may desire by appointing a successor trustee who will terminate the trust and distribute its corpus as directed in the trust indenture.

Although trusts are of many kinds, their principal objectives are to avoid probate, reduce taxation, and achieve legal immunity. Long ago, the wealthy learned how to protect their estates, keep them growing and inviolate generation after generation, and thus preserve their immense family fortunes for centuries. Now it becomes incumbent upon the members of the great middle class to preserve their lesser accumulations by the same procedure.

The most efficient way to accomplish this objective is through the creation of an irrevocable trust. This differs from a will, not only in that it is immune to probate, but also in that it is protected against law suits, attachments, or judgments aimed at the trustor. The trust is a separate entity created by contract; its assets cannot be seized, attached, or levied upon because of debts or obligations incurred by the trustor-creator. The trust differs from a will also in that the former must list each item of its property, whereas a will can consist of a blanket declaration such as that all assets, real and/or personal, owned by the testator, shall be left to certain heirs and devisees.

As a simple and practical example, let us assume that a married couple or the survivor thereof desires to convey a home or other property to a certain corporation or adult individual, while retaining control and the option of making different arrangements at any time. A revocable declaration of trust will then be prepared, stating the name and address of the owner together with the legal description of the property involved and declaring that the owner will continue to hold such property as trustee for the benefit of the person or organization named as beneficiary, who is usually also the successor trustee. Should such beneficiary be a minor, a successor trustee will be named who will manage, conserve, and finally distribute the property for the benefit of such beneficiary or beneficiaries as are named in the declaration or indenture of trust.

The instrument will then declare, under a series of subheadings, that the trustee reserves the right to mortgage or otherwise encumber the property described; to amend or revoke the same at will; to change any beneficiary; and that, in the event of death, the designated beneficiary will become the successor trustee, with all the powers formerly possessed by the creator-trustee, except where such successor trustee simply manages and conserves the property for the benefit of another.

The trustee may also include a provision in the declaration that should he become incapacitated, the beneficiary-successor trustee will become the interim manager and conservator of the estate.

In most cases, the declaration or indenture of trust will be filed with the authorities where deeds and similar instruments are recorded; however, this is not mandatory, but is considered desirable in order to establish beyond question the existence and validity of the trust.

The trustee then executes a quit-claim deed, in which the property is conveyed from himself as an individual to himself as trustee of the newly created trust. This document, which completes the transaction, must be recorded.

Should the owner change his mind about some provision in the trust or desire to terminate it entirely, he simply files an amendment to the declaration stating what alterations are desired; or he prepares a formal revocation of trust together with another quit-claim deed, in which the property is conveyed from the owner as trustee to himself as an individual; in which case the previous *status quo* is restored.

Many other types of trusts are possible, revocable or irrevocable. The latter are exempt from most gift taxation and from all estate or inheritance taxation until a final distribution of corpus is made; however, gifts made to others than spouses under revocable trusts are exempt from taxation only up to a certain limit. A spouse may receive one-half of a trustor's estate plus $134,000 (in 1978 and $175,000 in 1981) without gift taxation or any estate liability. A farm or a family urban business up to the value of $500,000 may pass from one generation to the next without estate taxation provided certain qualifications are met.

Trusts with a variety of substantial investments can be so created that a widow will receive the income therefrom during her lifetime; so that her children will receive it during theirs; and so that final distribution of assets will occur only in the third generation. Even an irrevocable trust can be renewed by the decision of the trustees with the consent of the beneficiaries.

Consider a man in his Sixties or Seventies whose accumulations total $3 million: he should lose no time planning the protection of such an estate, or even a smaller one. If he does nothing, the federal and state tax collectors may seize nearly one-half of it; but if he establishes a proper trust, this will continue unimpaired and inviolate; it can provide comfort and affluence for children and grandchildren. Its corpus may well double in ten or fifteen years; and it could ultimately be used as a college endowment or for some other beneficial purpose, instead of being taken and dissipated by bureaucrats or unworthy devisees.

F. SIMPLE TRUST ACCOUNTS AND SURVIVORSHIP DEEDS

There are simple procedures by which bank and savings and loan accounts can be exempted from probate. If John and Mary Doe have a passbook account or a certificate of deposit in a financial institution, this can be placed equally to the credit of both: which means that it is always at the disposal of either, and in case of death, it becomes the sole possession of the survivor without the necessity of doing anything. However, if one person wishes to retain sole ownership but also to make certain that money will pass to another without probate, he simply creates an account for John Doe a/t/f (as trustee for) Mary Doe — or whomsoever he wishes; it could be a son, a daughter, niece, grandson, friend, corporation, or any other entity. Upon his death, the asset will pass to the person or entity named, who or which will merely file a certificate of death in order to come into the property: no delay, no expense, no lawyers, no judges, no probate courts, no publicity, no possible contest over a will.

There is also a simple method by which people can avoid probate on real estate holdings without a will or a trust. For example, a man and wife should make certain that in the probable event that one predeceases the other, their residence or other property will not be subject to litigation. Lawyers and realtors

almost always prepare deeds which make the domicile community or commonly owned property, meaning that when one
dies, it will automatically be thrown into probate and half of it
will belong to the heirs of the decedent. All couples should guard
against such an eventuality; and if their deeds are not properly
drawn, they should quit-claim their homes (and/or similar
property) to a single third party, who will then convey them back
under a Joint Tenancy Deed to the couples *"not as* tenants in
common and not as a community property estate, but as joint
tenants with rights of survivorship." This wording is mandatory:
it means than when one dies, the other becomes sole owner
simply by filing a certificate of death with the proper authorities:
again, no delay, no expense, no lawyers, no judges, no probate
courts, no publicity, and no possible contest over a will.

By following these simple suggestions, a large portion of all
middle-class assets can reach heirs and survivors without delay,
expense, or difficulty. There need be no will for hungry or
disgruntled hopefuls to contest: in fact, they would have no
knowledge of the transaction until it is completed and
irrevocable.

Since life at all ages is uncertain and subject to accidents and
unexpected illness, we suggest that all those who have acquired
estates of any size plan for their protection and proper disposal.
And this applies particularly to older individuals, especially those
millions who, having attained their Psalmist's allocation of three
score and ten, have only limited expectations. Don't let
bureaucrats, lawyers, probate courts, or executors consume any
substantial portion of your life savings!

G.   EXEMPT SECURITIES

One of the most successful legal methods to avoid taxation on
current revenues is to invest in tax-exempt bonds, of which,
according to the 1977 *Statistical Abstract* (p. 267) $232 billion had
been issued by state and local governments alone in 1976, with
about $20 or $25 billion in new issues annually. There are also
many other categories of exempt securities, which now total
perhaps an equal amount. Instead of placing funds in banks or
savings and loan associations where taxable interest payments

average about five per cent, the person with $5,000 or $10,000 can purchase tax-exempts that pay anywhere from 6.5 to 8.5 per cent. In a few years, a thrifty middle-class individual can create an estate of $50,000, $100,000, or more. The most attractive features of such investments are (1) their high degree of security; (2) their immunity to taxation; and (3) their privacy and protection against disclosure. In short, this type of investment raises its beneficiary to membership among the financial elite.

When Mrs. Delphine Dodge received $56 million for her shares in her motor company, she invested her funds in tax-exempts, and was not required to file a 1040 on an annual income of $2,000,000. Had she earned $1,000 by taking in washing, she could have been sent to prison for failing to file.

H. INVESTING IN COMMERCIAL PROPERTY

In the preceding chapter, we discussed briefly the methods by which commercial property may be depreciated and the fact that large or substantial investors by the thousands are creating estates by this method and avoiding most or all income taxes during the process.

We knew one individual who, in the middle sixties, obtained land under a 100-year-lease agreement, which provided for proportional escalation in rentals in case of continuing inflation; the landowner, in return, agreed to subrogate his interest to that of any money-lender who might finance a 100-unit apartment building on the site.

By depositing $2 million of exempt bonds with a bank as security or collateral, it advanced the $2 million necessary to complete the facility at an interest of seven per cent. During the ten years required to depreciate the building, the owner received $2 million of tax-free income, which he invested in tax-exempts; he then sold it for $3 million, which would normally require a capital gains tax of $750,000. However, since he contributed a large sum to his own operating foundation, this gift completely cancelled his tax-liability. In other words, without actually investing a dime, he made a profit of $5 million.

Of course, the ordinary middle-class individual cannot operate in such a rarefied atmosphere. But he can certainly do what hundreds of thousands have done successfully: save some money from a personally operated business and then invest it in a self-liquidating commercial project, such as a warehouse, an apartment complex, a small shopping center, or something similar. We do not approve of single houses or other small units, for these need to be supervised directly by the owners and can be very troublesome and time-consuming. Instead, the project should be either a warehouse or store, from which the tenants mail in their checks regularly, operate under leases, pay for their own repairs and utilities, and are responsible for interior upkeep and maintenance. If the investment is residential, it should be large enough — at least 14 or 15 units — to justify a full-time caretaker on the premises who, in return for a tax-free apartment and a reasonable salary, will lease the units, collect the rentals, deposit the money in a bank account, make all minor repairs, and be responsible for the general operation.

Let us see how a new residential building with 20 unfurnished, 2-bedroom apartments, might operate:

Cost		$300,000.00
Down Payment		25,000.00
Debt Assumed with 15-yr. Amortization		275,000.00
Value of Land		30,000.00
Depreciable Improvements		270,000.00
Gross Income		65,000.00
Annual Expenses:		
Taxes	$ 8,000.00	
Debt Payments	18,333.00	
Utilities	10,000.00	
Average Interest	10,000.00	
Maintenance	5,000.00	
Caretaker Salary	3,000.00	
Vacancy Loss Ratio	3,000.00	
TOTAL		57,333.00
Cash Flow above Expense		7,267.00
Deductible Expenses		39,000.00
Depreciation		27,000.00
TOTAL DEDUCTIBLE		64,267.00
Taxable Income		733.00
Reduction of Debt		18,333.00
ANNUAL REAL INCOME		25,600.00

Barring a major depression or other similar development, an original investment of $25,000.00 will provide an annual return of more than 100 per cent; and, since inflation is almost certain to continue, the value of the property may double in terms of federal reserve notes in a few years, and thus the actual profit could be well in excess of $500,000 — all with very little time necessary for management or supervision.

A smaller investment which might be suitable for those who do not wish to plunge so deeply should produce proportional results. Of course, the investor must make a careful study of values and the future potential of the area involved before investing; for a mistake could be very costly. Two elements should be considered: (1) the site of the project; and (2) the prospects for the area in ten or fifteen years. However, what we have just described is today the basis on which tens of thousands of median fortunes have been erected.

E.   ESTABLISHING INDIVIDUAL TRUST ACCOUNTS FOR RETIREMENT

What began some years ago as a modest Keogh Plan permitting self-employed persons to establish their own retirement accounts has now been liberalized and expanded in Section 404(e)(1) of the IR Code to permit all such individuals to place up to fifteen percent of their earned income, but not in excess of $7,500, in such investments as annual deductible contributions The amount to which such a trust might grow in thirty or forty years is truly fantastic. A person who invests $125 a month or $1,500 a year at cumulative interest of eight per cent will have an inviolable corpus of $474,000 in forty years; then beginning at age 65, the retiree could receive a lifetime annuity of not less than $3,160.00 every month without reducing the principal; or, should he elect to exhaust the fund, he could draw $4,735.70 a month for 15 years or $4,171.80 during a period of twenty.

The following tables indicate how trusts of all sizes could grow and what they would provide at maturity and during retirement. And remember that these sums — unlike Social Security contributions — would be the property of the investor's: in case of death before the exhaustion of the corpus, the residue would go to heirs and devisees. Note the following:

WITH PAYMENTS OF $75 A MONTH			WITH PAYMENTS OF $250 A MONTH			
Years After	Amount Paid In	At Five Per Cent	At 7.5 Per Cent	Years After	Amount Paid In	At Five Per Cent	At 7.5 Per Cent
15	$13,500	$ 20,095	$ 28,788	15	$ 45,000	$ 66,982	$ 86,361
20	18,000	30,882	48,046	20	60,000	102,940	144,540
25	22,500	44,711	76,396	25	75,000	149,038	229,182
30	27,000	62,440	93,660	30	90,000	208,132	312,220
35	31,500	85,169	127,754	35	105,000	283,698	425,848
40	36,000	114,309	172,464	40	120,000	381,030	574,880

THE BENEFITS AVAILABLE FROM PERSONAL TRUSTS
(Monthly Payments)

Trust Size	By Taking Interest Only		By Exhausting Trust Fund at 8%		
	At 5%	7½%	In Ten Years	In Fifteen Years	In Twenty Years
$ 20,000	$ 83.00	$ 125.00	$ 250.88	$ 199.40	$ 175.65
40,000	208.33	312.00	501.76	398.80	351.30
100,000	416.66	625.00	1,254.40	997.70	878.30
200,000	833.38	1,250.00	2,508.80	1,994.40	1.756.50
500,000	2,083.61	3,125.00	6,272.00	4,965.00	4,391.40

The holder of such a trust account could begin drawing benefits at age 59½ or at 70, or any other established by law or personal preference. Any trustee dying before retirement would leave an irrevocable estate to heirs. The retiree could begin consuming the entire corpus during his lifetime in monthly installments, the amount determined by actuarial tables based on his expectancy; or it could be consumed during a given number of years; or, finally, he or she could decide to take the interest only, leaving the entire principal to heirs. But in every case, it would be a personal estate, which no other individual or any government agency could invade.

Of course, it would be of the utmost importance for Congress to establish a stable dollar, so that trusts of any size would not vanish into thin air because of the inflation now eroding our economy and threatening monetary chaos in the foreseeable future.

The exquisite beauty of the UTP (the Universal Trust Plan) — the real frosting on the cake — is that it would not cost the younger generation so much as one dime! The elderly would become treasured jewels, self-sustaining and honored, instead of the onerous burdens upon society they have now become.

In 1975, Congress added Section 219 to the IR Code, which permits any wage or salaried worker, not already covered by a specific retirement plan, to contribute up to fifteen per cent, but not in excess of $1,500 a year of deductible contributions to his own Individual Retirement Account (IRA). As with the self-employed, he becomes eligible to draw benefits at age 59½, or even earlier in case of disability.

Both plans are steps in the right direction as additions to, or replacements for, the present Social Security system, which provides no return for the payments made by the thirty per cent who die before retirement. The next progressive step would be for Congress to permit every individual who establishes his own irrevocable IRA to be excused from SS. The ultimate step will be to replace this entire system with a Universal Trust Plan, which would provide annuities for everyone at the same cost as Social Security, but with ultimate benefits three or four times as large and would do so FOR EVERYONE.

J. NEW ESTATE AND GIFT-TAX CREDITS

Some of the more important changes in the Tax Reform Act of 1976 deal with gift and estate taxes and especially the size of estates which may be transmitted from one spouse to another, to other heirs and devisees, and the size of closely held businesses which may pass within a family without taxation. The amount exempt when received by a spouse was half of the estate plus $60,000 between 1945 and 1976; when received by others, the exemption was limited to $60,000. For years, pressure to increase this limit kept increasing, as the buying power of the dollar continued to decline.

Under the new law (Section 2056(b)), no matter what the size of the estate, a spouse may receive as a marital deduction either $250,000 or one-half of the estate, free from estate taxation. In addition, one spouse may receive gifts without taxation from the other up to $175,000 beginning in 1981. The new law relating to estates and gifts, in addition to the marital deductions, provides

(1) That the exemption from taxation on all estates received by heirs and devisees (Section 2010(b)) is increased from $60,000 to $120,667 in 1977; to $134,000 in 1978; to $147,303 in 1979; to $161,560 in 1980; and to $175,655 thereafter. If the total estate does not exceed these totals, no estate return is required from the executor.

(2) That in a closely-held family business, including rental properties, or in the case of a farming estate, exemptions rise at once to $500,000 (Section 2032A). However, for such amounts to continue exempt, the heirs must remain as the operators of the family enterprise for fifteen years.

(3) That in case such farm-estate or other business does not have ready cash to pay the estate tax on amounts exceeding the exemptions, the heirs may be given a five-year deferral to begin payments, which may then be made in installments over a ten-year period.

(4) That unified rates be established for the taxation of gifts and bequests; and that all gifts made during the three-year period preceding death of testator be treated as portions of gross estates.

(5) That credits against gift taxes be increased (Section 2505(b) to the following amounts: $30,000 beginning July 1, 1977; $34,000 for the year 1978; $38,000 for 1979; $42,000 for 1980; and $47,000 thereafter. Since these credits make gifts untaxable to the same degree as estates, gifts are free from taxation on the same amounts as shown in paragraph (1) above.

These long overdue reforms will act beneficially to preserve literally millions of median proprietorships for heirs and devisees.

A. *Statistics of Individual Income* Dept. of the Treasury, 1971, p. 9.

Five   Why Are Audits Made?

IRS audits have no important purpose except as a means of collecting additional taxes and serving notice on taxpayers that they had better pay whatever the government demands. The agent may declare that a return has been chosen at random: don't you believe it! It was selected because it is that of a small businessman, which is itself sufficient motivation; involves commercial property; reports some financial transaction; claims allowances exceeding the accepted norm; is that of a taxpayer who has paid added levies in the past; or who is the object, for undisclosed reasons, of IRS harrassment.

If your return includes a business, the agent will seek to scrutinize all invoices, sales records, bank deposits, expenditures, cancelled checks, etc., to see whether he can discover some deduction not sufficiently documented or a discrepancy on which to hang an assessment. If your sales do not show proper markup over invoices, he will suspect underreporting of income; and should your bank deposits exceed your stated cash income — even if some of them consist of transfers from one account to another — he may assume without further evidence that you are guilty of tax-evasion, assess a huge liability, or even refer the case to Intelligence, which investigates fraud. At the very least, he will probably force you to prove that such deposits did not in fact constitute taxable income. Honest people have been hounded for years simply because money received in repayment of a debt had been deposited in a checking account. There are countless ways in which agents attempt to increase assessments. If, for example, any out-of-pocket expense is reported without a supporting cancelled check, this may be disallowed. The alert taxpayer, however, will dispute every questionable redetermination; and very often agents can be defeated completely.

To the independent businessman especially, the prospect of a "routine" audit, inflicted upon some three million Americans annually, can, with good reason, be extremely frightening; for it has led to the economic destruction of many thousands of citizens who were completely honest and who, to the best of their belief and knowledge, had paid every penny of tax due under the law. We know that the Service collects money from most of their examinations and that billions are extracted as a result of audits every year.

The Internal Revenue Service *Publication 556*, called *Audit of Returns, Appeal Rights, and Claims for Refund*, states that

> The vast majority of taxpayers are honest and have nothing to fear . . . An examination of such taxpayers' returns does not suggest a suspicion of dishonesty or criminal liability. It may not even result in more tax. Many cases are closed without change . . . and, in many others, the taxpayer receives a refund.

This is the bait; for what the taxpayer has to fear is not so much a criminal prosecution as the disaster which ensues when he is caught in some unsuspected trap or becomes the victim of IRS bluff.

In preparation for any confrontation, the taxpayer should obtain a copy of the Code from Prentice-Hall or the Commerce Clearing House, which also publishes the useful *Master Tax Guide*, written in simpler language. He should also learn how to look up court decisions in West's *U.S. Code, Annotated, Title 26*, or a similar compendium.

Unless you are in business for yourself, operate commercial property, are on the IRS computer as an easy victim, have received a substantial refund, listed unusually large deductions in your return, or consummated some business deal, it is not too likely that the IRS will take the time to audit your return. You can be sure, however, except in cases where the motivation is political rather than economic, that it will virtually never have any information concerning you except what you have submitted in your own reports. "Voluntary" compliance is required under penalties of fines and prison sentences for the simple reason that if the Service were required to discover relevant information through its own research, this would require literally hundreds of thousands of agents and informers at an expense so great that it would exceed the potential revenue. Nor, even so, could the reports thus obtained be accurate or complete.

The taxpayer may wonder why he should have to submit to an audit at all — answer questions, produce cancelled checks, and allow an examination of his books and records to verify deductions and expenditures reported under penalties of perjury. Do not these procedures constitute violations of the Fourth and Fifth Amendments? We can only say that although the government can no longer send a taxpayer to prison for declining to answer questions, it still arbitrarily disallows unverified deductions, recomputes the tax-liability on this basis, and seizes property unless the assessments are paid promptly, or an appeal is made for a redetermination through the administrative channels of the Service.

Although the Fifth Amendment specifically forbids the seizure of property without due process of law, the IRS does so thousands of times every day. And even though Section 6331(b) of the Code and many court decisions prohibit IRS seizure of real estate belonging to third parties who have no dispute with the Service or owe anything to the delinquent taxpayer, the Agency constantly violates this provision also. For example, it will commandeer, occupy, and change the locks on, a rented office, warehouse, or building housing a business where the tenant is allegedly in arrears in his taxes. It will then post the premises as government property. The owner would, in these circumstances, become a criminal trespasser subject to very severe punishment under Section 7212(b) if he entered his own building; he could lose thousands of dollars of income; and the IRS will rarely reimburse him unless he takes the Agency to court and obtains a judgment, which will apply only in the instant case. Under extreme pressure, the IRS may offer to pay the owner a minimum rental for the actual days it holds the premises, provided the owner can prove that he received no income for this period. The Agency will even declare that such taking and padlocking does not constitute seizure — that only the personal property within was "seized."

The reader will understand that IRS agents routinely make heavy assessments even when they have no authority to do so. Their statute contains many gray areas which are utilized to the fullest extent to assess deficiencies. Irrelevant sections of the Code may be cited as authority in the expectation that taxpayers will not know or understand them; others may be interpreted in whatever manner may be desired; agents have even been known to declare that the plainest words mean the very opposite of what they say.

Remember at all times that the IRS is an adversary — not a neutral appraiser; that its overriding purpose is to collect the maximum amount of money with the minimum expenditure of time and effort. The agent will therefore attempt to obtain quick consent agreements, under which substantial assessments will be paid; but no taxpayer should ever sign any document presented by an agent unless he is absolutely certain that no harm to himself will result. If an agent cannot obtain at least $100 for every hour he spends in audit, he is not worth his salt and will not be promoted; the taxpayer should therefore force the agent to spend the maximum of time for minimum returns.

The taxpayer facing an audit should, however, be encouraged by the knowledge that the IRS can no longer ride roughshod over its victims as once it did. For example, it can no longer send taxpayers to prison or fine them $10,000 for failure to answer questions or surrender their books and records; and it cannot compel them to prepare and submit the notorious ten-year Net-Worth Statement under threat of summary confiscation. Such reports, if made at all, must now be prepared by the Service through its own efforts; they are extremely difficult and costly; and are undertaken only in major cases, such as that which led to the resignation of Spiro Agnew from the Vice-Presidency.

Nor can the IRS obtain bank records or documents relating to tax-information from any third party as once it did. In fact, as we explain in a following chapter, it is now very time consuming to obtain such documents relating to the taxpayer who utilizes the protections written into the Internal Revenue Code. The Privacy Act of 1974, summarized in the official *Instructions for Form 1040*, reads in part as follows:

> The Privacy Act of 1974 provides that each Federal Agency inform individuals, whom it asks to supply information, of the authority for the solicitation of the information and whether disclosure is mandatory or voluntary; the principal purpose or purposes for which the information is to be used; the routine uses which may be made of the information; and the effect on the individual of not providing the requested information.

This notification applies to all returns made to the Internal Revenue Service, and requires it, whenever it seeks any information from a citizen, to state its precise authority for demanding it, whether disclosure is required under penalty, what the purpose may be in seeking it, and what may happen to the citizen should he refuse. Since the Service has routinely engaged in "fishing expeditions" by asking irrelevant questions or those unauthorized in its own law, and since it must now, whenever requested, cite definite chapter and verse from its law, the proper use of this Act will prevent most IRS attempts at prying into areas which are none of its business. If it asks any question beyond the minimum necessary to verify a deduction or an allowance or seeks any information not directly relating to the tax-liability, an appeal to the above-cited provision will usually stop it cold.

Six   The "Cooperative" Audit

As we have warned, the taxpayer must realize that if the
IRS levies a deficiency assessment, it will seize property
routinely unless deductions are verified or contested through the
administrative channels of the Service.

First, however, let us outline the preliminary steps which we
suggest. Upon receiving a call proposing an audit, the taxpayer
should tell the Agent that the proposed conference must occur at
a time and place convenient for him, such as his home or office. He
should also state that no arrangement will be made except in
writing.

Sometimes agents declare that audits must take place at IRS
headquarters. However, this rule can be enforced only when a
district court so orders.

If the taxpayer discovers, after a suggested appointment has
been made by the agent in writing, that the time is inconvenient,
he can write the agent by certified mail, return receipt requested,
asking that a different time, mutually acceptable, be arranged.
Such delays may well occur several times.

Agents sometimes appear unannounced at homes or offices
to make audits. If such an intrusion occurs, the taxpayer should
declare politely but firmly that no conference can take place
except by previous arrangement.

It should be understood that in this chapter we are dealing
with the taxpayer who wishes to avoid any serious battle with
the IRS; who is sure that he can verify all business expenditures
and itemized deductions; who has been careful to keep all
invoices, receipts, and cancelled checks; and who has studied the

sections of the IR Code which deal with his personal situation
sufficiently to feel certain of his position.

John B. Dougherty, who left the Service after fifteen years
to become a tax-preparer and who told his reasons for resigning
in the 1973 March-May issue of *Freedom,* published by the
Church of Scientology, offered advice which taxpayers can follow
and which, he declared, would make ninety-five per cent of the
Agency's abuses impossible.

(1) Never accept any verbal assurances, agreements, or
statements of fact or opinion from IRS personnel — compel them
to commit everything to writing;

(2) Do not sign anything the IRS places before you, unless
you are absolutely certain that doing so will not harm you;

(3) Never allow an IRS agent to copy or remove any paper,
record, or personal document of any kind.

Mr. Dougherty emphasized that every taxpayer has an
absolute right to these protections; that the IRS cannot refuse or
deny them; and that by using them, multitudes of taxpayers can
avoid irreparable damage. Mr. Dougherty declared that the IRS
has

turned into the largest secret police agency in the world . . . a
Monster . . . It pressures unnecessarily the small wage-earner,
the family man, and the small businessman, while large corporations are given only a cursory look. I saw life-savings
taken without a blink and businesses confiscated without due
process of law. And the word kept coming down, to get
tougher . . . tougher . . .

The inability . . . to pay was continually viewed as a
criminal evasion . . . I saw IRS agents drunk with power . . .
Some left the Service because of the pressures . . . one jumped
off the Golden Gate Bridge . . .

The IRS operates without judicial review, legal restraint,
or moral values. Its actions are limited only by what it believes
it can get away with . . . The 'little guy' is an easy target . . . He
can't afford to spend $500 to keep from paying $200 . . . He
simply pays the IRS without question. Billions are collected in
this way . . . Internal Revenue fears only one thing: public
opinion . . .

The taxpayer should never permit the agent to go on a "fishing expedition"; nor should he permit access to his bank records or others in the custody of a third party, such as a bookkeeper, a lawyer, or an accountant. In this refusal, he is fully protected by Section 7609, which was added to the Code in the Tax Reform Act of 1976.

In his preliminary correspondence with the IRS, the taxpayer, while offering to cooperate in every legal demand, will insist firmly that he receive in writing an exact list of what information is desired, why it is wanted, and the exact authority on which any demand for information is based. He should also study carefully *Publication 556*. At the conference, therefore, he will have the necessary data on hand, but nothing else should be offered or supplied.

In 1976, the Congress passed a special law providing that if an audit does not increase tax-liability, then, if the Service re-examines the same taxpayer in either of the next two years and again no increase results, the IRS must make reimbursement for the entire cost of proving the taxpayer's innocence. For this reason, *Publication 556* added the following statement in 1979: "We try to avoid unnecessary repetitive examinations of the same items, but this occasionally happens. Therefore, if your tax return was examined in either of the two previous years for the same items and the examination resulted in no change to your tax liability, please contact the person whose name and telephone number are shown in the heading of the letter you received as soon as possible. The examination of your return will then be suspended pending a review of our files to determine whether it should proceed." Note that there is no reference to the law passed by Congress. The same Publication continues: "You may represent yourself at your appeals conference, or you may be represented by an attorney, a certified public accountant, or an individual enrolled to practice before the Internal Revenue Service." The taxpayer should always be on the alert for every trick practiced by the IRS. The unmentioned hook in this is that any person representing a taxpayer must be given power-of-attorney: which means that he can make any deal with the IRS he may wish or betray his client completely.

I have heard IRS agents declare that no one except such persons as those enumerated above can even be present during an audit or examination: but if he makes such a statement, he should be required at once to produce his authority for so saying from the IR Code; and he will be lying, ignorant, or bluffing: for *Publication 556* states explicitly: "You may bring witnesses to support your position;" which means that other persons may not only be present, but may also aid orally in your defense.

When, therefore, the agent arrives to conduct the "examination," you will have present a lawyer, an accountant, or a tax-preparer if you wish and if any of these are involved in your tax-situation. However, if you have prepared your own return, we suggest that you have two or three friends present who will not only act as witnesses but who may corroborate your position. If the agent objects to their presence, read his own law to him: which will demonstrate that you are not to be bluffed in any way.

Although there can be little doubt that the IRS has hidden microphones in their offices when interrogations take place there, it is a well-known fact that its agents are inordinately terrified of tape recorders when used by taxpayers in their homes or offices. It seems that they make so many misstatements, are enmeshed in so many contradictory declarations, fail to answer so many pertinent questions properly, that to them it is almost a matter of life and death to remain unrecorded. They can always deny an undocumented statement, but if it is on tape, they cannot squirm out of it. We therefore suggest that the ordinary taxpayer have a recorder on hand: and if the agent refuses to converse unless it is turned off, the taxpayer will follow his own judgment. However, should the agent follow this course, he should be asked what provision in the Code or what official Regulation forbids the use of tapes. The agent may declare that the Agent's *Manual* forbids the use of recorders, except in cases of criminal investigation: that they can be used only by special permission; and that he has no authority in the matter. However, we know of various instances in which taxpayers have used recorders; and the transcript of the UNITED STATES OF AMERICA VS. MELVIN AND PEGGY JOHNSON (which we reproduce in the APPENDIX) can be cited to advantage; and the taxpayer is wholly within his rights if he refuses to continue a conference unless recorded by himself as well as by the agent.

Concerning his own taxes, financial situation, and potential tax-liability, the taxpayer should volunteer no information; he should supply only what is essential to verify expenditures or deductions claimed on the 1040. Whenever an agent makes a statement or requests any information beyond this basic require- ment, the taxpayer should quote the Privacy Act and force him to reveal his authority and quote the pertinent provision in the Code on which he relies. For example, if he should ask what allowances you give your children, what your wife spends for clothes or cosmetics, whether you own any tax-exempt bonds or other securities, or how much you spent for a car or a vacation, you should tell him to cite the number of the Code Section which authorizes him to demand this information; if he cites one, then force him to read it in your presence and that of your witnesses in order to discover whether he really possesses such authority. NEVER ACCEPT ANYTHING AN IRS AGENT TELLS YOU AT FACE VALUE. If the IRS has taken possession of *your* real estate to impound personal property belonging to your tenant, tell him to cite Code authority for such action. If he wants to change your method of bookkeeping, force him to read the law to you — do not accept some regulation from a little book which he may pull out of his pocket.

If, during the conference, the agent asks for verification of a deduction for real estate taxes, he should be shown the receipted tax bill and the cancelled check used to pay for it. The same procedure will apply in regard to items involved throughout the audit.

Let us consider the taxpayer whose car has been damaged beyond repair in an accident not covered by insurance: if the agent tries to reduce the casualty deduction to the wholesale level, the taxpayer will rightly insist that the retail price at a new car agency be permitted. If his wife has lost her diamond ring or injured it in an accident, he is entitled to a loss equal to its present value, not merely its original cost. If he makes a gift to a church or a charity of any tangible or intangible asset, he may report the present retail or market value thereof as a deduction.

Since the number and variety of disputes that can arise during and following an audit are almost infinite, we cannot describe or enumerate them. Every case is different and the taxpayer must know how to defend himself in his own situation; nor should he, under any circumstances, agree to any redetermination of tax-liability in favor of the government unless this is absolutely inescapable.

The watchwords which the taxpayer should observe are these:

(1) Conduct all pre-examination communications in writing.

(2) Insist that the conference take place at a time and place convenient for *you.*

(3) Before the conference or examination begins, insist on an exact list of what is to be verified or justified, and why.

(4) Do not engage in any discussion beyond these limits or permit any examination of documents except those necessary to verify deductions or expenditures.

(5) Have a CPA, lawyer, bookkeeper, or other witness present if any of these were involved in the preparation of your return.

(6) Have a tape recorder on hand, and insist on using it.

(7) Never volunteer any information.

(8) Keep copies of all correspondence with the IRS.

(9) Never permit any agent to copy any documents or remove them from your premises or possession.

(10) Never sign anything an IRS agent places before you, unless you are certain that no harm will result to you.

(11) Compel the agent to cite his authority for demanding any information or for anything he proposes to do.

(12) Never agree to the payment of a single dime of additional tax unless this becomes absolutely necessary.

(13) Never permit a second examination of the same material.

(14) If you are audited and found to be without tax-liability one year, refuse any audit during the following two

years.

(15) Whenever the IRS proposes an audit, take immediate steps to protect any records which may be in the possession of any third party, such as a lawyer, CPA, or accountant.

Should the IRS make disallowances or "adjustments" which result in increased tax-liability but which seem in any way questionable, prepare to pursue your defense through a conference at the district level, then in the Appellate Division, and, if necessary, even in the Tax Court. Remember, that you are simply pitting your time against that of the IRS. The Service is desperately desirous of obtaining the greatest possible amount of money with the smallest possible expenditure of time and effort. It should be your objective to force it to work overtime for every dollar it may extract from you.

Seven	The Contested Audit

A. THE PRELIMINARY STEPS

We consider now the taxpayer who has made a "proper" return and paid all taxes he believes due, but who, nevertheless, has decided that he will not submit to a "routine" audit.

When such an individual receives a telephone call that his return is to be audited, he should follow the procedure suggested in the previous chapter in regard to written communications and to a conference to be arranged at a time and place convenient for him. He will also probably take immediate steps to protect documents in the custody of any third party which could have any bearing on his tax-liability — particularly those in the possession of a bookkeeper, accountant, or lawyer.

One of the favorite ploys of the IRS has been to serve its Form 2039A, or "vest-pocket" summons, upon recordholders, demanding that documents pertaining to a taxpayer be surrendered, including those of other persons who have had any financial dealings with him. Bankers have often acceded to this because of possible retaliation, without even notifying the individual involved when ordered to produce for examination

all books, records, papers, and memoranda, of whatever nature or kind relating either directly or indirectly to accounts open or closed, in the name of John Q. Taxpayer, his wife, Mary, or their children, for the period shown. These records include by way of illustration, and not by way of limitation: signature cards, ledger sheets, (or numbered histories of accounts from computer printouts), deposit slips, deposited items, paid withdrawal checks, escrow statements, safe deposit rental and entry records, applications, financial statements, payment records, contracts, trust deeds, notes, certificates of deposit, cashiers checks, bank drafts, and cashed items; for checking, Savings, Loan, Safe Deposit, Escrow and Trust Accounts; correspondence file, forms 1099.

In the past, bank depositors have tried to protect themselves from such intrusion by an appeal to *Reisman v. Caplin* and other court decisions; however, in *Bisceglia*, the Supreme Court sanctioned what amounted to a "fishing expedition"; and in *Miller* it declared that the taxpayer had no reasonable expectation of privacy concerning the records in a bank pertaining to his accounts. Furthermore, the courts had held consistently that documents in the custody of accountants and lawyers must be made available to the IRS on demand.

Now, however, all this has become obsolete because Section 7609 of the Tax Reform Act of 1976 provides protection for all records held by third parties that never existed before. All such records are now placed under a protective umbrella. If the IRS issues a summons to any third-party record holder, notice of such summons must be sent within three days to the taxpayer and at least fourteen days before the contemplated examination is to occur; and this must be accompanied by full instructions as to how compliance may be delayed or prevented. The summons must, furthermore, identify the taxpayer and contain specific information enabling the record-holder to locate the desired material easily. The IRS must pay any expenses involved.

The taxpayer needs only to send a letter by certified mail, return receipt requested, to the record holder and to the IRS stating that such examination is not to be permitted without the consent of the writer. If the IRS then appeals to a U.S. District Court for a show-cause order, the taxpayer has the right to intervene before any determination may be made; and also to appeal an adverse decision to the United States District Court of Appeals.

In the meantime, the IRS cannot enforce any assessment or initiate any action.

We should note that this revision of IRS law was the result
of combined pressure exerted by some fourteen thousand banks
and it indicates that important reforms can be attained if enough
people demand them with sufficient determination and logic.

We should note also that if, at any time, the IRS turns over
its investigation of a taxpayer to its Intelligence Division — as it
is called — this becomes a criminal procedure, and the IRS is
required to read the Miranda Warning to the taxpayer, who will,
from that point on, naturally refuse to answer any questions asked
by an agent.

B. THE ADVICE OF "A. PATRICK HENRY"

Among various recommendations made to taxpayers concerning their rights and conduct during a first conference with an
auditing agent, we note the suggestions in a pamphlet entitled
How to Protect Yourself from the Internal Revenue Service,
published under the alias of A. Patrick Henry. The author
declares that his approach "has been carefully researched in the
law, court cases, and the Constitution and is guaranteed to
accomplish the intended results." The law, he declares, makes
adequate provision for the protection of the taxpayer under the
Constitution; and he should retain the perjury line in the 1040 for
his own protection. We are told:

> In completing the return and signing it as prescribed in the
> form, you have taken an oath that your return is correct.[A] Once
> you have taken this position, under our system of law, which
> holds that a person is innocent until proven guilty, you have
> actually placed the burden of proof that your return is incorrect
> on the IRS.

Therefore, whenever the IRS audits a return, the taxpayer is
entitled to the Miranda warning; however, IRS agents do not
even carry Miranda cards. Nevertheless, a taxpayer should not
fear them, for they cannot themselves make an arrest or enforce
a summons or a subpoena. The pamphlet continues:

> At the time appointed for the revenue agent to visit you,
> be certain that you have at least three witnesses present; also

a tape recorder with the microphone in such a position that it will pick up all the voices of those present.

If the agent objects to the presence of witnesses and/or friends, he should be told that even according to IRS publications it is the taxpayer's privilege and RIGHT to have them; that there is no law, rule, or regulation against the use of a tape recorder; that several Federal District Court judges have sanctioned its use; that it is going to remain; that the conversation *will* be recorded; and that otherwise there will be no conference.

When the agent explains that he is there simply to examine records in order to veri*y* deductions and expenditures, the taxpayer should declare that he has already made his return under penalties of perjury as provided in the tax form and that any omission or misstatement would constitute fraud, a criminal offense. It is therefore not necessary to verify any statement made therein; any attempt to establish the contrary is the responsibility of the IRS — for this is constitutional law, any provision in the Agency Code to the contrary notwithstanding. The author then continues:

> There is no provision in the Code making it mandatory for you to prove the figures on your income tax return.
>
> The Internal Revenue Code provides that the IRS has the right to examine your records. This must be done, however, only with your permission or by a court order.
>
> If your return *is* incorrect, you can invoke the Fifth Amendment to the Constitution and you cannot be compelled to furnish any evidence or give any testimony that may tend to incriminate you — even with a court order.
>
> The courts have stated time and time again that although the Congress does have the power to tax, this power is limited by the provisions of the Constitution; therefore, the enforcement of any of those provisions is limited by the protective elements of the Constitution.

So far A. Patrick Henry.

C. OUR SUGGESTED CONDUCT DURING CONFERENCE

We cannot too often emphasize that, even according to official IRS documents, it is the right of the taxpayer to have present, not only a tax-preparer, a CPA, or a lawyer, but also other witnesses and spokesmen. As we have also noted, IRS agents are exquisitely paranoid over the use of tape-recorders. However, contesting taxpayers will ordinarily insist on their use. If an agent flees in the face of such a mechanism, the taxpayer is within his rights in declaring that no audit may proceed without it. Furthermore, as we have already pointed out, the taxpayer can cite U.S. VS. MELVIN AND PEGGY JOHNSON, the transcript of which is reproduced in the APPENDIX.

We repeat that a taxpayer should never volunteer information, but say only what is essential concerning his financial situation. At the same time, he should obtain the agent's name and service number to make certain of his identity; if he leaves any documents, he should be required to inscribe his own name upon them; and any statement he makes should be fully recorded, as indicated above.

If the agent states that the taxpayer has violated any IRS law or regulation, he should be required to produce and leave with the taxpayer a copy of such law or regulation. This is the taxpayer's abolute right under the Privacy Act.

During any conference which occurs in a home or office, the taxpayer should observe the agent closely to discover any unauthorized procedure. If it seems that illegal assessments are being proposed; or if, after an audit, the IRS continues to harass the taxpayer, he should prepare a statement carefully describing his experiences, which he may decide to send to his two senators, his congressman, and to the chairman of the Senate Appropriations and Finance Committee. The IRS finds it highly embarrassing to explain to a member of Congress why an innocent constituent is being hounded. If the taxpayer has a good case, it might even be expedient for him to air his complaint in the newspapers, there being nothing that the IRS fears more than derogatory publicity.

When the agent arrives, he should, therefore, find himself face to
face, not only with the taxpayer, but also with friends serving as
witnesses. After a polite introduction, the following conversation
might ensue:

"Who are these people?"

"Friends of mine."

"Why are they here?"

"To observe what happens."

"Will they identify themselves?"

"That is not necessary." (They may decide to give their first
names only.)

"Are they lawyers or CPAs?"

"No."

"Have you given them power-of-attorney?"

"No."

"Well, then, they cannot be present."

"Oh, yes, they can because *Publication 566* specifically states
that a taxpayer may have witnesses present at any conference or
audit hearing." This may prompt the following question:

"Do they intend to say anything?"

"Possibly."

"They are not permitted to do so."

"Oh, yes, they are; for the same publication states that I may
"bring witnesses to support my position." The taxpayer then
shows the agent the passage and reads it to him, at which point
the agent becomes aware that he is dealing with an informed and
intelligent person; and he will be very careful in what he ways.
He may also notice the tape-recorder: "Is that turned on?"

"Yes."

"Our conversation may not be recorded."

"What law, regulation, or provision in the Internal Revenue
Code forbids the use of a recorder by a taxpayer?"

The agent will hedge and evade the issue: "We do not permit
the use of recorders during audits, for it is prohibited in our
Manual."

"Does the *Manual* have the force of law enacted by
Congress?"

"You can't have the recorder turned on during our conversation."

"Why not? What is the IRS afraid of?"

"Nothing — it is simply contrary to policy."

"Well, sir, it is *my* policy to make sure that nothing said here can later be denied or altered and therefore I must insist on making a recording. Some of my friends have had denials of fact from IRS agents in the past. I am perfectly willing to have you bring your recorder and to use it; and I am sure you use recorders when audits are made at headquarters. Besides, a U.S. District Court judge has declared that taxpayers have a legal right to use tape recorders."

At this point, the agent may refuse to continue. However, should he go on, he will demand that the taxpayer produce all records for examination, to which the taxpayer will reply:

"Is it not true that I have already filed my 1040 under penalties of perjury and that any omission from it or misstatement in it would constitute fraud, punishable by fines and imprisonment?"

"I am only conducting a routine audit; this is not a criminal investigation. I only want to help you make a correct return."

"You have not answered my question: does not my signature under the perjury line mean anything? Have I not declared under penalties of prosecution that I have told the truth and the whole truth? If you discover any falsity, can I not be prosecuted criminally for fraud?"

"I am only here to verify your deductions and allowances."

"I have already made these under penalties of perjury."

"Well, I am required to examine your supporting documents in order to determine the correctness of your report."

"Will you explain the meaning of the perjury line above my signature? Does not the IRS state that if this is crossed out, the return is regarded as if it had not been made at all, even if it contains full disclosure and all taxes are paid in full?"

"I am only required to verify your deductions and examine your documents to make sure that you have not made any errors. This is only a civil proceeding."

"You can discover any mathematical error in your office. And let me ask you this: will you give me an affidavit signed by

the District Director that nothing found in an audit of my return
will ever be used in a criminal prosecution?"

"I am not engaged in any criminal investigation — I am here
only to verify your deductions and to examine documents to make
sure that your return is correct."

D.   CITING THE CONSTITUTION AND THE SUPREME COURT

At this point, if the agent is still willing to continue, the
taxpayer may inquire: "Do you believe in the Constitution?"

"I believe that the Supreme Court is the proper authority to
interpret it — I am not a constitutional lawyer."

"Then you *do* believe that if the Supreme Court makes a
constitutional ruling or renders an interpretive decision, this
should be binding upon everyone?"

"Oh, yes."

If the recorder is in operation, the taxpayer has now
achieved a powerful advantage; and he continues:

"Do I understand correctly that the principal purpose in
making an audit is to verify deductions and expenditures and that
this examination of my records could result in an increased tax-
assessment?"

"If your records do not substantiate your deductions and
allowances, it will be necessary for me to make an adjustment in
your tax-liability."

"What happens if I decline to turn over my records for such
an examination?"

"You will leave us no alternative except to recompute your
tax as if there were no allowances or deductible expenditures."

"What you are saying is that if I do not prove my innocence
by establishing the truth of the statements already made under
penalties of perjury, you will tax me exactly as if I had not
reported any deductions or allowances?"

"That is the law as passed by Congress."

"Is it not also true that if I have no records to show that I
have made the reported expenditures, I can be indicted for fraud,
tried, convicted, and sent to prison?"

"If you are guilty of fraud, you may refuse to turn over the

the records by claiming the Fifth Amendment privilege."

"But only by subjecting myself to the possibility of prosecution."

"Fraud might be implied."

"But if you assess a tax for non-compliance, is not that also a fine — in effect, the punishment for a crime?"

"No, that is only a civil penalty."

Now begins the frontal attack: "You have stated that the Supreme Court is the only authority empowered to interpret the Constitution and that its opinions and decisions are binding upon everyone — I assume you mean both the taxpayers and the IRS: is that not correct?"

"Well, yes."

"Are you acquainted with the case of *Boyd v. United States*, decided February 1, 1886?"

"No."

"Well, in that case the Supreme Court explains specifically the Fourth and Fifth Amendment rights and privileges of all taxpayers and citizens of the United States. It declares that no federal agency may use any records it obtains from a taxpayer under threat of punishment to assess a tax or to increase a tax; nor may it base any such assessment on a refusal to surrender records. I can read what the Supreme Court said if you want to hear it."

"It doesn't make any difference what it said in a case decided almost a century ago. And I can tell you that when you filed your 1040 Form under penalties of perjury, you waived all constitutional immunities anyway. It is as simple as that."

"Well, then, you are saying that I could assert my constitutional privilege by not filing any return at all?"

"No, because you make the return voluntarily and because you need only tell the truth."

"What do you mean, voluntarily! Doesn't Section 7203 say that if I don't file, I can be sent to prison for a year and fined $10,000 on each count? And didn't the Supreme Court say in *Boyd* that even when records are produced by court order, they cannot be used to reassess a tax?"

"Well, maybe the records involved there were not required

in the first place — I don't know the case."

"Oh, yes, they were: they related to imported goods on which the law required that import duties be paid. When they were smuggled in, there was a double breach of law. Yet the government could not use the invoices when produced under court order to assess a tax."

"I don't know about that. Anyway, we have other Supreme Court decisions which say that the Internal Revenue Code and procedures are constitutional."

"Well, then, if the Supreme Court contradicts itself, does the IRS have authority to accept only those decisions it likes? And is not the taxpayer given the same privilege?"

"I'm not here to discuss all this. All I can say is that if you refuse to verify your report, we will have no choice but to recompute your tax as if there no allowances or deductions."

"In other words, the Internal Revenue Service declares that I am a perjurer and pays no attention to provisions in the Constitution or to Supreme Court decisions it does not like."

"Sir, I have a job to do; and that is to examine your records and verify your deductions and allowances. As far as I'm concerned, the Internal Revenue Service and Code are constitutional and the Supreme Court has so stated repeatedly. If you don't agree, you should go to your congressmen and ask them to change the law or you should take us to court and see whether you can get different decisions."

"My friend, I am only trying t tell you that the Supreme Court has declared that it supports the Constitution when it says that no one shall be deprived of life, liberty, or property without due process of law; and that no one needs to go to a law school to understand what the Constitution says."

"Well, there is no use arguing about this any more; are you, or are you not, going to show me your records so that I can verify your expenditures?"

"I have no economic objection to so doing, because I know that under penalties of perjury I have made full disclosure and, to the best of my knowledge and belief, have paid all taxes due. But I do not know what trickery the IRS may use to injure me. However, if you will bring me an affidavit signed by your district director that you will never use anything you may find in an examination of my records in a criminal proceeding, I will permit you to examine them."

"This is only a routine audit; it is not a criminal investigation."

"Your answer is not responsive. I have already made my return under penalties of perjury. A misstatement or omission would constitute fraud, punishable by fines and imprisonment. If I am guilty of crime, the burden of proof is on the government. I am not required to help you to prove any such charges or allegations, and therefore I will not permit you to examine my records without a court order. If you arbitrarily disallow any of my deductions, you will have to list them and explain why you have done so. I will contest every redetermination all the way to the Tax Court."

The taxpayer may then continue:

"You know that you cannot arrest me for refusing to turn over my records in spite of what is written in Section 7203 of the Internal Revenue Code; for these provisions have been outlawed by the courts. I have nothing to hide and nothing to fear. I have paid all my taxes. You will not be able to obtain any money from me no matter how much time you spend, unless you can catch me in some irrational trap in the Code. I will not permit you to go on a fishing expedition or to enmesh me in some snare of which I know nothing. And you will get nowhere by trying to bluff me into believing you can tax me because of some non-existent law or provision that you may invent. I will not cooperate with you in twisting the law so that you may be able to extort money from me that is not due or more than is due."

In all probability, this will conclude the conference; and the agent in total frustration, and perhaps boiling with rage, will be forced to return to his office without having accomplished his mission. What he may do thereafter, we discuss in the next chapter.

E. SUMMARY

Although we do not imply by any means that a taxpayer can rid himself of the IRS by the above method, we know of instances in which it has accomplished that result. At the very least, the Agency will have been foiled in its attempt to obtain a quick assessment; it will realize that every dime to be collected from such an individual will come only after long and expensive effort. Remember that unless agents can produce at least $100 for every hour they spend on a taxpayer's audit, their efforts are counterproductive.

Nevertheless, if the IRS is persuaded that a substantial sum can be obtained, it will probably pursue the taxpayer by all means provided in its cumbersome statute. However, if it cannot visualize such success, it may forget the whole thing, and the citizen will have removed the IRS millstone from his neck forever. It cannot spend huge quantities of time doing research where potential returns are insubstantial or non-existent.

It is obvious that, after making "routine" audits, the IRS not only violates the Constitution, but also such Supreme Court decisions as *Boyd* countless times every day. It now — and finally — admits that private papers may not be obtained under criminal sanctions; but if these are not forthcoming, the Service simply disallows deductions, and proceeds to assess a deficiency without evidence that additional tax is in fact due. Actually, what it does is far worse than what was strictly forbidden in *Boyd.* Returns are filed under penalties of perjury — a situation not involved in that dispute; the taxpayer, who has already laid himself open to heavy fines and imprisonment under duress because of possible fraud, must permit the IRS to examine his records in violation of the Fourth Amendment in order to prove his innocence, or his property will be confiscated without due process of law in violation of the Fifth; if the audit reveals fraud, his own testimony or lack of it is used to prosecute and convict, also in violation of the Fifth. Since property seizure without due process constitutes a criminal penalty equally with the deprivation of life and liberty, the IRS violates *Boyd* as well as the Fourth and Fifth Amendments every time it disallows a deduction simply because a taxpayer declines to verify it in order to prove his innocence.

We repeat that as long as the IRS continues to seize property without due process of law even when no tax is due, the taxpayer should never trust an agent or believe anything he says: and only multi-millionaires and large corporations can afford to place implicit confidence in tax-specialists. Every man is his own best friend; and those in the middle-income levels must learn how to defend themselves if they wish to preserve what they have.

And we repeat also that it is a very serious error to pay a few hundred dollars when a questionable assessment is made because doing so is easier or cheaper than to resist: for by such submission, the taxpayer becomes an annual target for extortion. If he had defeated the IRS soundly after his first audit-confrontation, in all likelihood, he would have been left alone thereafter.

It has been common practice for the IRS to bill taxpayers for amounts varying from $50.00 to $300.00 under some vague formula which does not specify why the money is owing: and we believe that in this way thousands have paid money not due. In order to avoid the cost of counsel or the expenditure of time necessary to delve into the mystery, many people have simply remitted. No greater mistake, however, could be made; for if the taxpayer had insisted on an explanation, this would eventually have been forthcoming and he could probably, at least in most instances, have been able to demonstrate that no money was due. Any taxpayer who pays under such circumstances becomes, in fact, a kind of co-conspirator with the Internal Revenue Service. He can and should contest every penny of any item which is not established as owing beyond all shadow of doubt.

Although we are confident that the procedures suggested herein are effective and know that they are available to all taxpayers, we must again caution them that their use may not only frustrate the IRS but also provoke reprisals. However, the taxpayer will be completely within his legal rights; and it has been demonstrated thousands of times that those who cannot be bluffed or intimidated into submission fare much better than do those who knuckle under without resistance.

By refusing to permit agents to examine books or records during a first conference, the taxpayer is only wagering his own time against that of an agent; and even if the IRS continues to pursue the taxpayer, he still has at his command all the rights and privileges under administrative law that he had in the first place. In short, he has nothing to lose but some of his time; he has a world to gain.

In the next chapter we describe what the taxpayer can or must do if the IRS decides to use all its power to compel the production of books and records in order to collect additional taxes which the taxpayer is convinced are not owing.

A.   This is not quite accurate; for returns are not sworn to before a notary public or other officer.

B.   We should note that it is quite unlikely that any agent will engage in any debate with a taxpayer concerning the constitutionality of any law; agents are warned against doing so.

Eight   The Administrative Process

A. ON GUARD!

After the first confrontation with the IRS is completed without an audit or an examination of his records, the taxpayer may await the next step with some pertubation. Actually, the IRS has three choices: (1) to drop the whole procedure; (2) to seek a court order to compel the surrender of books and records; or (3) to disallow all deductions, and assess a deficiency on the basis of such recomputation.

Although an IRS agent could himself discover by means of a telephone call whether a certain medical bill had been paid to a hospital, he probably will not do so; instead, he will insist on placing the burden of proof on the taxpayer by requiring him to produce bills, receipts, and cancelled checks. Remember, that under Section 6331 of its Code, the IRS is empowered to seize property *by any means;* it can take the furniture from your home, the equipment out of your office, the books from your library, the coal out of your bin in the midst of winter — all without due process of law. It can seize deposits in savings and loan accounts, commercial deposits in checking balances, the family automobile, and the equity in an insurance policy; it can force anyone who owes the taxpayer money to pay the same to the government. It can place a lien on your home; if you own personal commercial property — such as printing equipment — the building in which it is located can be padlocked, posted as government premises, and its contents sold within a few days at a small fraction of its value; the owner may even be charged a fee for conducting the sale, since this may not produce enough to pay the cost of the auction. Even though, under its own law, it may not sell your childrens' school books, the clothing from your back, the tools of your trade up to a value of $250.00, and certain other articles (Section 6334(a)), it may seize these also and hold them in ransom.

B. THE DEFICIENCY LEVY

If the IRS decides to pursue the taxpayer after he has refused an examination of his records, it may simply recompute his tax on the basis of total disallowance without supplying details or explanation, send him a levy based thereon, write him that he is entitled to a conference in the district office to discuss the dispute, and inform him that unless he takes affirmative action, levies upon his assets may begin within ten days. To ignore this ultimatum may result in serious consequences.

To such a letter, we suggest that the taxpayer reply by certified mail, return receipt requested, stating that all arrangements must be made in writing. He should state that, since the letter redetermining tax-liability contains no information as to what disallowances are made or why, this information must be available in detail at any future conference. To such a demand, the IRS must comply.

If the taxpayer discovers that it will be inconvenient for him to meet an appointment, he can request a postponement. However, in the situation now under consideration, we believe it wiser for him to agree to an appointment, preferably in his own home. He should also insist that the use of a tape-recorder be permitted (as it has in various instances of which we know). He will also insist on a complete Bill of Particulars before any discussion occurs; and he will not answer any questions in regard to his taxes or exhibit any records until he has had time to study the recomputations proposed by the government. He will simply declare that he is in complete disagreement with the findings that have been made and that he intends, if necessary, to pursue the administrative process through the Appellate Division and even to the Tax Court.

This statement will initiate a course of action which will be largely under the control of the taxpayer. *Publication 556* explains:

If you don't agree with the changes proposed by the examiner, and if the examination was made in an Internal Revenue Service office, you may request an immediate meeting with the supervisor to explain your position to him. If agreement is reached, your case is closed. If agreement is not reached at this meeting, or if the unagreed examination was made outside of an Internal Revenue Service office, we will send you (1) a transmittal letter notifying you of your right to appeal the proposed adjustments within 30 days, (2) a copy of the examination report, explaining the proposed adjustments, (3) an agreement or waiver form, and (4) a copy of Publication 5, *Appeal Rights and Preparation of Protests*...

This is the well-known Thirty-Day Letter; if the tax is not paid or appealed within this period, the IRS may give the taxpayer the Ten-Day Letter, after which the seizure of property can or may begin.

Note that if an examination is made outside an IRS office and it proposes "adjustments," it must explain them fully in its Transmittal Letter. In most cases, the taxpayer should, as a matter of course, reject the IRS proposals and proceed to the next step in the administrative process. He now has in his possession a full explanation of precisely what changes the IRS proposes. This is for his benefit, because it invalidates any "fishing expedition" and limits the auditing agent's examination to certain specified items. And this sets the stage for the only audit that may take place during any one year under Section 7605(b).

Now for the first time, the ordinary taxpayer who insists on his rights faces an audit. However, he has neither relinquished nor diminished any of his immunities because of what has happened; and he will now reiterate to the Service that all arrangements must be in writing; that the audit will take place only at a time and place convenient for him; that any demand that he bring his records to IRS headquarters for examination can be enforced only by an order from a United States District Court; that he will discuss only specified items which must be listed for him in writing previous to the meeting; and that the conference must be tape-recorded.

As already pointed out, when the agent arrives for the audit, the taxpayer has a right to have with him not only a CPA, a lawyer, or a bookkeeper, as well as his tax-preparer, but also friends who will serve as witnesses and even as spokesmen. What we stated previously about tape recorders is equally applicable. We repeat that only one examination of records may be made for any one year; the agent may not make a copy of any document; nor may he remove anything from the taxpayer's premises. Should he state otherwise or declare that he must copy the records in order to reconstruct the taxpayer's return, he should be required to reveal his authority from the Internal Revenue Code; and he should be told that if he wishes to reconstruct the return, he must do so entirely on the basis of his own independent research.

Should the agent refuse to continue the audit unless he is permitted to remove or copy the taxpayer's records, he has waived all right to make such examination; and should the IRS then seek an order in a U.S. District Court to obtain and copy them, the taxpayer will have a perfect defense. Since he has offered complete cooperation, the IRS can have no further claim; and it cannot demand the right to examine the records for any one year a second time. Under no circumstances should the taxpayer recede from this position, even if he must appeal all the way to the Circuit Court of Appeals.

Whenever an IRS agent demands information, he should be required to state his requests in writing, explain exactly what is wanted and why, and declare what the punishment will be for failure to comply. He should also tell the taxpayer to what use the information will be put — all this as mandated in the Privacy Act.

As we have emphasized, the taxpayer should never volunteer any information during a conference. And we repeat that he should say as little as possible concerning his income, expenditures, or tax-liability. However, he should observe the agent closely for any errors he may commit and be prepared to utilize these to the fullest extent. Since the taxpayer will have an official letter stating what data is required, he will be prepared to produce cancelled checks verifying business expenditures and other deductions and allowances; he will also have W-2 forms indicating wages or salaries received, as well as 1099 forms, showing income from interest, dividends, and commercial rentals. If he is a businessman, he will have invoices and records of receipts; if he has commercial property, he will show depreciation schedules and cancelled checks verifying his expenses. No other information will be made available; non-deductible outlays are none of the agent's business and if he seeks to investigate these, he should be so informed.

During the audit, the taxpayer should contest every adjustment proposed by the agent to increase tax-liability. He should be knowledgeable concerning depreciation rates, permissible deductions of all kinds, and oppose the agent on every item. Sometimes he can win points during the audit-interview. Nevertheless, the agent, anxious to make the largest assessment possible, will make as many disallowances and other "adjustments" as he can, and the taxpayer should be prepared to reject his proposals and proceed to the next step in the administrative process.

In due course, the agent will send the taxpayer his detailed proposals, which brings the dispute to the conferee or supervisory level in the district office. Here there is no further examination of records — there is simply an argument over the proposed adjustments.

Publication 556 states:

> If, after receiving the examination report, you decide not to agree with the examiner's findings, we urge you to first appeal your case within the Service before you go to court ... If you do not want to appeal your case within the Service, however, you can take it directly to court, i.e., the Appellate Division.

Publication 566 continues:

> We now have a single appeal level within the Service. Your appeal from the findings of the examiner is to the Appeals Office in the Region. Conferences are conducted on as an informal a basis as is possible. If you want an appeals confer-

ence, address your request to your District Director in accordance with our transmittal letter to you. Your District Director will forward your request to the appeals office, which will arrange for a conference at a convenient time and place and will discuss the disputed issues fully with you or your representative.

So, according to your own preference, you may bypass the District Office Conference, and go directly to the Appellate. In order to obtain "prompt and full consideration by the appeals officer, you may need to file a written protest with the District Director." However, if one has already been filed in his office, this need not be repeated. Such a document is not necessary before going to the Appellate Division if the amount in dispute is less than $2,500 or if the taxpayer's examination was conducted by correspondence or by an interview at the Internal Revenue Office.

Publication 556 states that the written protest should be submitted within the thirty-day period and should contain:

1. A statement that you wish to appeal the findings of the examiner to the Regional Director of Appeals;

2. Your name and address;

3. The date and symbols of the letter of transmittal mentioned previously;

4. The tax periods involved;

5. An itemized schedule of disputed adjustments;

6. A statement of facts supporting your position in any factual issue; this must be supported by a statement made under penalties of perjury;

7. A statement outlining the law or other authority upon which you rely.

Publication 556 continues:

You may represent yourself at your District Conference or Appellate Division hearing, or you may be represented by an attorney, certified public accountant, or an individual enrolled to practice before the Internal Revenue Service. If your representative attends a conference without you, he or she may receive or inspect confidential information only in accordance with a properly filed power of attorney or a tax information authorization.

In this manner, the IRS, like the Inquisition of the Middle Ages and the English Star Chamber Courts, keeps a tight rein on lawyers and CPAs; those enrolled to practice before the IRS can be decertified at any time. Furthermore, the taxpayer must trust his economic life to the discretion of his representative, who therefore can make any deal he may see fit. However, note this: "You may also bring witnesses to support your position" — which means that they may not only listen, but also speak on your behalf — a right which the IRS constantly denies, but one upon which every taxpayer can and should insist.

Note also that the IRS demands that *you* cite law and authority — information which the Agency rarely volunteers unless it can be used against the taxpayer. However, under the Privacy Act, this duty falls squarely on the shoulders of the IRS.

Beyond the Appellate, the taxpayer can go to the Tax Court, the Circuit Court of Appeals, and even to the United States Supreme Court by one route; by another, he can pay what the IRS demands, appeal for a refund, finally obtain a jury trial in a United States District Court, from which he may go to the Court of Appeals and again, even to the Supreme Court.

C. SUMMARY OF APPEAL PROCEDURES

Let us summarize the techniques available to the taxpayer for the protection of his assets:

(1) By following the method we outline in the previous chapter, he can delay the first conference perhaps for weeks or months or even frustrate the IRS completely in its attempt to obtain information.

(2) Should the agent, rebuffed at the first conference, be instructed by his superiors to pursue the taxpayer through administrative channels by disallowing deductions and making other "adjustments," the taxpayer should demand a complete Bill of Particulars, explaining in detail the reason for each "adjustment."

(3) When the IRS sends its detailed recomputation and

explanation, the taxpayer should request that an appointment for
any conference be made in writing and that it occur at a time and
place convenient for the taxpayer.

(4) When the agent appears at home or office, he may face
also the taxpayer's CPA, lawyer, bookkeeper, or tax-preparer, as
well as witnesses and a tape recorder. The agent must explain
why any changes are proposed, and cite specific authority.

(5) The taxpayer will not refuse to verify deductions and
allowances, but he will not permit the agent to remove any record
or document from the premises or make any copy thereof.

(6) If the agent will not continue the examination with a
tape recorder in operation or without being permitted to copy
records, the taxpayer can logically take the position that he has
cooperated fully but that the IRS has waived its right to make the
examination. Any denial of this position should be contested in
the courts.

(7) After the agent's redeterminations are forwarded to the
taxpayer in written form by mail, the latter has thirty days in
which to demand a Conferee hearing in the district office, where
he should expect most of the agent's findings to be upheld. All
communications should still be in writing. At this point and under
certain conditions, the taxpayer may prepare his written Protest,
or this may await the next step — that at the Appellate level, or
in the Small Business Court, which we discuss below.

(8) At the Appellate conference, he may find that the IRS is
prepared to settle at thirty or forty cents on the dollar of the
original assessment.

(9) If the taxpayer is dissatisfied with the terms offered at
the Appellate level, he will go to the Tax Court, a procedure we
discuss in the next chapter.

(10) Even if he is not satisfied with the results there, he can
furnish bond and go directly to the Circuit Court of Appeals
without paying the tax demanded.

(11) In the meantime, three or four years may elapse; the
assets of the Taxpayer remain safe and under his control; the IRS
will have spent time and energy which would ordinarily be
devoted to disputes involving huge amounts of money; and it may
well end up collecting nothing at all.

Equipped with pertinent information, the taxpayer can present his case convincingly to the Tax Court before one of its sixteen judges and do so without the aid of a lawyer. If millions of angry Americans were to do this, the tribunal would become so clogged with cases that they could not be processed for years or even decades; and, until final adjudications are reached, the IRS cannot lay its hands on a dollar's worth of the taxpayer's property.

An old pro in this game once suggested to this writer that a great many taxpayers should take somewhat inflated allowances on their returns, which, if disallowed, could be disputed through the Appellate all the way to the Tax Court. In his *Freedom Fighter* of April 6, 1977, Rene Baxter goes a step further and suggests that taxpayers inflate their deductions to the point where no tax-liability will exist; before these can be disallowed in the Tax Court, several years will have elapsed and its administrative machinery will have ceased to operate. Suppose a million taxpayers were to report overgenerous deductions for casualty losses, sales and other taxes, depreciation on property, gifts of tangible goods to charity, the value of an office in the home, expenses incurred in making a living, exemptions for a neighbor's children who frequent the taxpayer's home, etc., — and the IRS will be compelled to end the whole ridiculous system of exemptions, deductions, allowances, etc., and permit, instead, every taxpayer to take a full cost-of-living allowance or, in the case of large incomes, a substantial percentage reduction in lieu thereof from Adjusted Gross Income, with additional allowances for high medical expenses. At a single stroke, this would eliminate most of the disputes which now rage between taxpayers and the IRS.

D. IRS PROCEDURES AND THE SMALL CLAIMS COURT

Effective as of December 30, 1970, a division of the Tax Court was established to handle claims not exceeding $1,500, in which the taxpayer is authorized to represent himself in an informal conference; however, experience has demonstrated that he will be faced by crafty government lawyers; and often he has discovered too late that no appeal is permitted. Most taxpayers

will therefore use caution in going this route. Should they decide
to do so, Instructions will be found on pages 76-79 of *The Rules of
Practice and Procedure*, published by the Tax Court. On the
following pages, we reproduce the chart showing Income Tax
Appeal Procedures in the Internal Revenue Service and the
petition form used in making an appeal to the Small Claims Court.

E. TYPES OF DISPUTES AND ISSUES

Phil and Sue Long of Bellevue, Washington, forced the IRS
to disgorge a great many of its secret documents, in one of which
we find that the Service recognizes three principal categories of
disputes. The first is the "split-issue," i.e., one which, if tried in
court, would probably result in a complete victory for one of the
litigants. In such cases, the IRS evaluates its chances of winning;
if this is estimated at thirty per cent, it will hold out at first for
one hundred, seventy-five, or fifty, but will settle at the lower
figure if the taxpayer remains firm. If it believes it will lose in
court against a determined taxpayer, it may drop the case
entirely.

"Pattern Issues" are those which occur most frequently and
involve less than $2,500. Here the IRS seeks to avoid all
precedent-setting decisions by compromises at the Appellate
level, where it secretly predetermines what its floor settlement
should be. Here the IRS officer and the determined taxpayer face
each other like antagonists in a duel. The latter may offer a
twenty-five or thirty per cent settlement, while the former
demands seventy-five. It is not really a question of right or
wrong; it is not even a question of whether money is actually
owing: the crucial point is how far the taxpayer will go to defend
himself and what his chances of ultimate success may be. The IRS
knows that it will cost him time and/or money to appeal; but it
knows also that an adverse decision in the Tax Court or in a
United States District Court, and especially in the Court of
Appeals, will be highly damaging to itself. IRS statistics show
that on the Appellate level, the average case of this type is
settled at about forty per cent of the original assessment.

The third type of dispute consists of "Prime Issues," in which
the IRS has not obtained a sufficient number of favorable

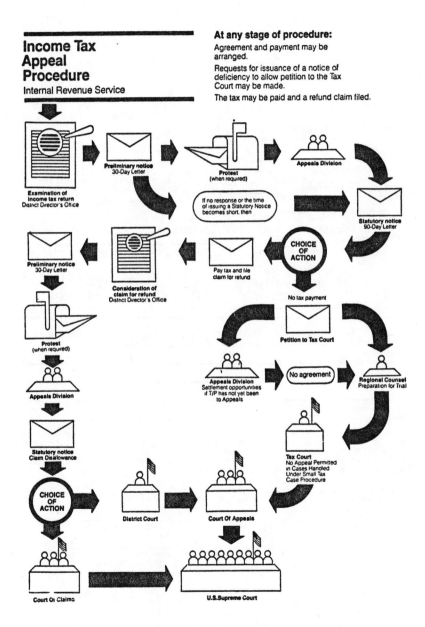

Income Tax Appeal Procedure
Internal Revenue Service

At any stage of procedure:

Agreement and payment may be arranged.

Requests for issuance of a notice of deficiency to allow petition to the Tax Court may be made.

The tax may be paid and a refund claim filed.

Examination of income tax return
District Director's Office

Preliminary notice
30-Day Letter

Protest
(when required)

Appeals Division

If no response or the time of issuing a Statutory Notice becomes short, then

Statutory notice
90-Day Letter

CHOICE OF ACTION

Pay tax and file claim for refund

Consideration of claim for refund
District Director's Office

Preliminary notice
30-Day Letter

No tax payment

Petition to Tax Court

Protest
(when required)

Appeals Division

Appeals Division
Settlement opportunities if T/P has not yet been to Appeals

No agreement

Regional Counsel
Preparation for Trial

Statutory notice
Claim Disallowance

Tax Court
No Appeal Permitted in Cases Handled Under Small Tax Case Procedure

CHOICE OF ACTION

District Court

Court Of Appeals

Court Of Claims

U.S. Supreme Court

PETITION
UNITED STATES TAX COURT

)
————————————————)
Petitioner(s)   )
v.   )   Docket No.
Commissioner of Internal Revenue,)
Respondent   )

PETITION

1. Petitioner(s) request(s) the Court to redetermine the tax
deficiencies for the year(s) _____, as set forth in the notice
of deficiency dated _____, A COPY OF WHICH IS ATTACHED.
The notice was issued by the Office of the Internal Revenue Service
at _____
        City and   State

2. Petitioner(s) taxpayer(s) identification (e.g. Social Security number(s)) is (are) _____

3. Petitioner(s) make(s) the following claims as to his tax
liability:

Year	Amount of Deficiency in Dispute	Amount of Addition to Tax, if Any Disputed	Amount of Overpayment Claimed

4. Set forth those adjustments, i.e., changes, in the notice of
deficiency with which you disagree and why you disagree.

_____

_____

_____

_____

Petitioner(s) request(s) that the proceedings in this case be conducted as a "Small Tax Case" under Section 7463 of the Internal Revenue
Code of 1954, as amended, and Rule 172 of the Rules of Practice of
the United States Tax Court. A decision in a "small tax case" is final
and cannot be appealed by either party.

_____   _____
Signature of Petitioner (Husband)   Present Address

_____   _____
Signature of Petitioner (Wife)   Present Address

                _____
                Signature and Address of Counsel, if retained
                            by Petitioner(s)

decisions but believes it can be victorious in the instant case. Concerning the nature of such disputes, it divulges no information; and when they reach the Appellate Division, the IRS reverses itself and insists on litigation. This is what happened to my astute friend in Detroit, where the Court determined that vacant lots owned by an investor may be treated as if they constitute a store inventory; and in another case, in which it was decided that taxes paid on depreciable commercial property may not be deducted by a new owner as a business expense during the first year, or more, of ownership.

F. THE SENSITIVE CASE

Again and again, the IRS *Manual* repeats the admonition that *before* any action is taken against a taxpayer who may develop into a "sensitive case," a full report must be sent to a Regional Commissioner, who will determine what action, if any, is to be taken.

In general, a Sensitive Case is one which, should it become known, would be of considerable public interest and could result in embarrassment because of publicity in the mass-media, or enquiries from members of the Congress, the Treasury Department, or even the White House. As an extremely sensitive case, Miss Vivien Kellums was left completely alone, nor did the IRS attempt any collection of taxes from her, although she never made any report or paid a penny in income taxes during the last eight years of her life on known, substantial revenues.

The *Manual* Supplement No. 12 C-35 states that if the taxpayer is a major political figure, such as a U.S. representative, the governor of a state, the mayor of a large city, or a prominent party official; if he is a close friend of any such personage; if he is a foreign dignitary; if he is seriously ill; if he is a nationally or internationally known businessman, racketeer, union official, religious figure, entertainer, or sports figure; if a club with a large or influential membership or an organization of importance, influence, or national scope is involved; if any segment of the mass-media is concerned; if the person has received prior public attention because of his criticism of the IRS; or if he has attained national publicity or interest — then any

investigation is virtually certain to become a "sensitive case." If
any of these criteria apply, agents must not proceed until a full
report has been sent to, and permission received from, the
Regional Commissioner. The *Manual* declares that since the

> issuance of a statutory notice of deficiency gives the taxpayer
> the opportunity to file a petition, this creates publicity . . . in
> deciding whether a statutory notice is to be issued, the over-
> all effect on the Service is considered, rather than the amount
> [of money] involved in a particular case.

Agents are warned to be extremely careful

> in the case of a celebrity, or a religious, charitable, or edu-
> cational organization, which, if docketed, would result in un-
> favorable publicity or embarrass the Service.
>   All necessary security measures must be adopted to pre-
> vent premature or unauthorized disclosure of any Service plan
> or activity in cases which, because of their sensitive nature or
> obvious need for secrecy in carrying out particular phases of
> the planned activity, must be handled in confidence.

Therefore,

> If . . . the conferee believes the case might require a sensitive-
> case report, he should discuss the case with his supervisor
> prior to taking any further action. The supervisor will decide
> whether a report should be prepared.

It might be advisable for some of those taxpayers who find
themselves in the toils of the IRS and who are convinced that
they do not owe what is demanded, to prepare a full statement of
their disputes; have it reproduced in quantity; send copies to the
newspapers, the radio, and T-V commentators, and especially,
with covering letters, to their members of Congress. Some
senator or representative may write the IRS, asking for an
explanation, which it will find very difficult to ignore and even
more embarrassing to answer.

G. CONCERNING THE FREEDOM OF INFORMATION

The IRS *Manual* states that

the citizens in a democracy are entitled to know about the manner in which their government operates; that the Freedom of Information Act requires that each Federal agency shall make available for public information and copying

all material used by it. Yet on August 25, 1967, only three months after the Act became effective, Commissioner Cohen published a restrictive amendment; and on February 27, 1970, Commissioner Thrower ordered almost all *Manual* material removed from public reading rooms. Mr. Long discovered that unless a taxpayer knows the exact technical title of a document, the IRS simply denies its existence. Sometimes it has changed the name or the numbering of documents and when the new ones were unknown to inquirers, their existence was denied. However, those who know how to use the Act, can obtain an immense amount of information.

H. THE APPELLATE DIVISION

Each of the regional offices of the Internal Revenue Service operates an Appellate Division; these are located in Atlanta, Chicago, Cincinnati, Dallas, New York, Philadelphia, and San Francisco. The regional offices have service centers in Austin, Kansas City, Memphis, Holtsville (New York), Cincinnati, Andover (Mass.), Ogden (Utah), Chamblee (Georgia), Philadelphia, and Fresno, California. Appeals may be made through any district office to the nearest of the above; and branch offices have been established in most of the larger American cities. After the taxpayer has mailed his formal PROTEST AND BRIEF (which should be sent by certified mail, return receipt requested), he will in due course receive notice setting a date and place where his dispute will be considered.

When we arrive in the more rarified atmosphere of the Appellate, we find that the IRS has established various categories of cases. It prefers to settle all disputes at the lowest level if this is possible; and unless it has a very strong case, it is extremely anxious to avoid a showdown in the Tax Court, where decisions become precedents of record and where disputes are settled for an average of about thirty per cent of original assessments. If the taxpayer has a strong case and refuses to compromise (which is like plea-bargaining where an accused person pleads guilty to a lesser offense in order to avoid a trial on a more serious charge) the IRS may reduce its demands drastically or drop them entirely at the Appellate level.

When the taxpayer's confrontation with the IRS reaches this point, he should be well prepared with a solid brief, citing in particular those court decisions which uphold and maintain his position and contentions.

On the following pages, we reproduce a model of what could have been used by the used-car dealer, mentioned in a previous chapter, in his brief to the Appellate Division. This should be prepared carefully and written on the special kind of paper used in such pleadings; at least four or five copies should be made; and they should be bound in the heavy, blue bindings used for this purpose. Any stationery store handling such materials can supply whatever is necessary.

The appellant then relates the origin and history of his business; his method of keeping books; how he has sold cars with small down payments; how he handled his own paper and guaranteed that he would retain the contracts; and how, at all times, he not only made complete and accurate financial reports to the Internal Revenue Service, but also paid all taxes which, to the best of his belief and knowledge, were legally due. The IRS never questioned Appellant's method of keeping books during the first seven years of operation. He then describes his first encounter with the IRS agent, who appeared, according to his own statement, simply to make a routine audit, from which the Appellant would have nothing to fear. He then describes the agent's method of auditing; his arbitrary refusal to consider the statements of the Appellant; his failure and refusal to cite any authority in IRS law or court decisions for his determinations; and the Appellant's utter frustration in attempting to arrive at any reasonable adjustment with this auditing agent.

(The above portion of the Written Protest and Brief will probably cover several pages.)

The Appellant then explains that after being audited by Agent Smith from the District Office in the city of _____

P R O T E S T   A N D   B R I E F

Appealing the determinations, in the case of the
present Appellant, from the determinations of Agent
John Smith and Conferee James Jones of the District Conference Staff in the Office of the Internal Revenue Service located in the City of _____
in the State of _____.

                    (Signed) John ч. Taxpayer
                              Address

          (Place here the date and symbols of
          the Transmittal Letter containing the
          proposed but disputed adjustments.)

          (State here the tax periods involved
          in the dispute.)

      STATEMENT OF ADJUSTMENTS BEING PROTESTED

Year   Deficiency   Penalty

19__ $19,326.70 $9,663.35
19__   19,219.22   9,609.61

        TOTAL   38,545.92   19,272.96

        GRAND TOTAL $57,818.88

      CONCISE STATEMENT OF ISSUES INVOLVED

1. What method of accounting will be used to compute
    Appellant's tax-liability for the years 19__ and
    19__?

2. What amount of tax is due using this method?

3. What method of accounting should be used in past,
    present, and future years which will most clearly
    reflect true income of this Appellant?

      GENERAL STATEMENT OF FACTS

   In appealing this case to the Appellate Division of the
Internal Revenue Service, Appellant states:

   Under penalties of perjury, I declare that I have examined the statement of facts presented in this Protest in
the accompanying schedules and statements, and, to the best
of my knowledge and belief, they are true, correct, and
complete.

in the State of _____, he was ordered to change his
method of accounting for income tax purposes from cash to
accrual, under which promissory notes were to be reported fully
as immediate cash income, although the money received
constituted only perhaps ten or twenty per cent of the contract
price, much of which might never be realized at all because of
discounts or defaults. This determination by the agent resulted in
an assessment of $38,545.92 for the two years audited. The agent
also assessed a fraud penalty of fifty per cent, which was simply
incredible since there had never been any fraud or even any
allegation of fraud.

Since the assessment of Agent John Smith was sustained by
Conferee Jones, the Appellant has been unable to obtain any
redetermination of his tax-liability in the District Office of the
Internal Revenue Service.

I. ARGUMENT IN THIS CASE

Since the Internal Revenue Code confers upon every retail
merchant, including used-car dealers, the absolute right to
continue on the same cash basis used previously as long as this
reflects true income, Agent John Smith and Conferee James
Jones were guilty of inexcusable error in ordering this Appellant
to change his method of bookkeeping from cash to accrual.

In making this determination, Agent Smith and Conferee
Jones cited sections 446(b) and 481 of the Internal Revenue Code
as their authority. However, in the instant case, both agent and
conferee are guilty of gross error, for the sections cited by them
completely negate and overthrow their position; in fact, they
fully support and maintain Appellant's unquestioned right to
continue in the same method of accounting for income-tax
purposes that he has previously used. Section 446(a)(b) and (c) of
the Internal Revenue Code of 1954, as amended, reads as follows:

(a) GENERAL RULE. — Taxable income shall be computed under the method of accounting on the basis of which
the taxpayer regularly computes his income in keeping his
books.

(b) Exceptions. — If no method of accounting has been

regularly used by the taxpayer, or if the method used does not clearly reflect income, the computation of taxable income shall be made under such method as, in the opinion of the Secretary or his delegate, does clearly reflect income.

(c) Permissible methods. — Subject to the provisions of sub-sections (a) and (b), a taxpayer may compute taxable income under any of the following methods of accounting —
    (1)   The cash receipts and disbursement method;
    (2)   an accrual method;
    (3)   any other method permitted by this chapter; or
    (4)   any combination of the foregoing methods permitted under regulations prescribed by the Secretary or his delegate.

It would constitute the height of absurdity for the Agent or the Conferee hereinbefore mentioned to hold that subsection (b) above gives them the power arbitrarily to order this Appellant to change his method of accounting from cash to accrual, because they must first demonstrate either that Appellant had no method of accounting or that the cash method does not clearly reflect his true income, which they cannot do; and they must show that the accrual method would do so, which is impossible. Furthermore, such arbitrary action would be in complete violation of other sections of the Code, which we now reproduce.

Section 453(a), covering installment-sales, applies precisely to Appellant's situation and confers upon him the absolute right to report as current income only that portion of sales contracts received during the fiscal year which constitute profit over and above the investment in the merchandise sold:

(a)   Dealers in Personal Property —
(1)   In General — Under regulations prescribed by the Secretary or his delegate, a person who regularly sells or otherwise disposes of his property on the installment plan may return as income therefrom in any taxable year that proportion of the installment payments actually received in that year which the gross profit, realized or to be realized when payment is completed,

bears to the total contract price.

This section is so clear that it cannot possibly be misunderstood; and the right of the retailer to report his income on this basis is supported and enforced by literally hundreds of court decisions which we are prepared to cite when necessary and all of which maintain Appellant's absolute right (1) to remain on the same basis which he has used during seven years of previous business without challenge from the IRS; and (2) to report as current income only that portion on sales contracts actually received during the current year. No judicial fact is more firmly established than that a note does not reflect or constitute income until it is redeemed or payable in full. (Cf. Paragraphs 623 and 624 in the *Master Tax Guide* for the year 1977.) For example, if a man accepts a promissory note of $1,000, to be paid six months or a year later, for work done or goods sold, this is reportable as income, not when the note is signed and received, but only at the date of redemption and payment. In order to be reportable income, funds must be entirely at the disposal and command of the recipient, such as interest credited to a savings and loan account, but not withdrawn, by the owner.

Here the Appellant may quote paragraphs 661 and 662 of *The Master Tax Guide*, which clearly declare his rights to report as income only that portion received from installment sales in excess of the cost of the item sold. Thus, if a car that cost $400.00 is sold for $800.00, no taxable income is involved until after the original sum is fully recovered, which is merely return of capital.

Appellant will point out that since, under the proposed accrual method, he would be required to prepay the tax on the entire amount of possible profit from installment sales, this would be contrary to all existing law or established procedure. Unpaid balances on Appellant's notes or accounts receivable are not only unavailable as income — there is, in fact, no certainty that these payments will ever be made. Some of them will surely default and others will certainly be settled at discounts. Appellant's capital is invested in equipment and inventory, and most of potential income is untaxable because it is only a recovery of investment.

At this point, Appellant may well ask whether it is a principal objective of the United States government to drive a hard-working businessman into destitution by twisting and violating the plainly stated provisions under which the Internal Revenue Service operates?

The Appellant now notes that as authority for his determination, the Agent also cited Section 481 of the Internal Revenue Code. However, this also completely refutes and demolishes the position taken by the Agent and the Conferee; it categorically forbids the very action they have taken:

SEC. 481. ADJUSTMENTS REQUIRED BY CHANGES OF METHOD IN ACCOUNTING.

(a) General Rule — In computing the taxpayer's taxable income for any taxable year (referred to in this section as "year of change") —

(1) if such computation is under a method of accounting different from the method under which the taxpayer's taxable income for the preceding taxable year was computed, then

(2) there shall be taken into account those adjustments which are determined to be necessary solely by reason of the change in order to prevent amounts from being duplicated or omitted, except there shall not be taken into account any adjustment in respect to the taxable year in which this action does not apply unless the adjustment is attributable to a change in the method initiated by the taxpayer.

It is obvious that this section has no relevance to Appellant's case and it certainly does not confer upon the IRS the power to make an assessment against him: it applies only when the taxpayer's method of accounting has been altered by his own initiative. This Appellant's method of accounting has never been changed, nor has he tried to initiate any such change. On the contrary, he is insisting on keeping the same method he has always used, but which the IRS is now attempting to alter illegally by duress.

Appellant now declares that he can, and upon request will,

cite dozens of court cases which support his right to continue on a cash basis and which completely demolish the position of the Agent and the Conferee in making their assessments against him.

Appellant will point out, finally, that Agent Smith and Conferee Jones assessed against him not only an erroneous and illegal tax, but also a fifty per cent penalty, which can be imposed only for fraud, as set forth in Section 6653(b) of the Internal Revenue Code, although no charge of fraud was ever made or alleged. On the contrary, Appellant has at all times made complete and accurate disclosure and has timely and fully paid all taxes due. This assessment for fraud therefore constitutes the crime of knowingly demanding money not due and therefore should be punishable under Section 7214 of the Code with a fine of $10,000, imprisonment for five years, dismissal from employment, and the requirement that restitution be made to the aggrieved party by summary execution.

In view of the above indisputable facts and because the Internal Revenue Code itself as well as all applicable tax and case law nullifies the determinations and assessments made by Agent Smith and Conferee Jones, Appellant prays that their assessments, penalties, and determinations be set aside and nullified.

Please advise when and where conference with the Appellate officer will take place.

Respectfully submitted
John Q. Taxpayer
City,   State

At the conference, the taxpayer will, of course, bring with him not only his brief and a copy of the Code, as well as *The Master Tax Guide*, but also numerous citations of court decisions which sustain his position. He must also show by his demeanor and presentation that he has no intention of acceding to anything which does not fully represent his rights. In a case like that outlined above, he should never agree to any compromise settlement which would require him to pay so much as one dime of the original assessment. Since the law and the court decisions are clearly and overwhelmingly on his side and since the IRS demands were obviously based on pure bluff and a total misinterpretation of its own law, we doubt that the Agency would dare take a dispute of this kind to any court of record, where an adverse decision would put a summary end to its harassment of used-car dealers. We know that it often tries to make its Code say the opposite of what it does say; it routinely ignores Appellate decisions, which are not recorded or published; and it tries to take the position that adverse decisions in the Tax Court, in the United States District Courts, and even in the Circuit Courts of Appeal apply only to the individual cases covered. However, it instantly cites lower-court opinions favorable to itself as if they were ultimate authority. Nevertheless, by failing to appeal when it loses in the Tax Court or the United States Courts of Appeal, it acknowledges the error of its position; and any determination by a court of record, favorable to the taxpayer and cited by him, will usually compel the IRS to discontinue its harassment.

J. BEYOND THE APPELLATE

If the taxpayer refuses the terms offered at the Appellate level, the IRS will send him what is known as the Ninety-Day Letter, or STATUTORY NOTICE OF DEFICIENCY, which requires definite action within this period, or the seizure of assets may and probably will occur. Upon receiving this, he faces a crucial decision: (1) he may pay the tax assessed and thus close the case; (2) he may pay the tax, sue for a refund through the District Office, and finally obtain a jury trial in a United States District Court; or (3) he may, by petition, proceed directly to the Tax Court, which has headquarters in Washington and branches in sixty-three cities and is manned by sixteen judges who serve fifteen-year terms. Although this Court is created by provisions in the Internal Revenue Code (Sections 7441-47), it claims to be entirely independent (*Publication 556*); we are told that it has "no connection with the Internal Revenue Service," a statement which some people find hard to believe.

In the next chapter, we describe the procedures to be followed in making appeals to the Tax Court; in Chapter Ten, the techniques to be pursued in going to a U.S. District Court of Appeal.

A. Perhaps even in this Protest and Brief the Appellant should cite pertinent passages from certain court decisions which support his position.

Nine   The Battle in the Tax Court

A. THE PRELIMINARY STEPS

Although an appeal to the Tax Court is a more elaborate undertaking than that involved at the Appellate level, many determined taxpayers, even without benefit of counsel, have gone there successfully. The *pro se* litigant should understand, however, that he must submit a PETITION within a ninety-day period and in accordance with a specified format. This, however, is neither impractical nor very difficult because a handbook called *Rules of Practice and Procedure: United States Tax Court* (available from the government Printing Office in Washington, D.C., for $1.10 or free from the Tax Court itself) enables any alert and intelligent layman to prepare his own PETITION.

If a taxpayer declines to pay the assessment determined in the Appellate Division, he will, as we have noted, receive a Ninety-Day Letter, or STATUTORY NOTICE OF DEFICIENCY from the District Director of Internal Revenue, together with documents containing (1) An Explanation of Adjustments; (2) A Computation of Allowable Deductions; and (3) the Waiver of Restrictions on Assessments.

When this letter is received, the taxpayer must take specific action: he must either pay the assessment proposed, or prepare to follow the available administrative procedures in order to dispute the claims and demands of the Service.

On the following page we reproduce a Ninety-Day Letter, or STATUTORY NOTICE OF DEFICIENCY; the name of the tax-payer has been changed because of fear of future harassment and persecution.

119

Internal Revenue Service
District Director
Date: Month, Day, Year

CERTIFIED MAIL

Department of the Treasury

Tax Year Ended and Deficiency:
Penalty Code Section 6651 (a)

April 30, 1969	$0,000.00	$000.00
April 30, 1970	0,000.00	000.00
April 30, 1971	000.00	000.00

00-000000
Association for Political Freedom, Inc.
10,000 Anystreet
Anytown, California 90000

Person to Contact: Code 000-00-000
A. B. Beaurocrat
Contact Telephone Number:
(213) (000-0000)

Gentlemen:

This letter is a NOTICE OF DEFICIENCY—as required by law—that we have determined the income tax deficiencies shown above. We regret we have been unable to reach a satisfactory agreement in your case. The enclosed statement shows how the deficiencies were computed.

If you do not intend to contest this determination in the United States Tax Court, please sign and return the enclosed waiver form. This will permit an early assessment of the deficiencies and limit the accumulation of interest. The enclosed self-addressed envelope is for your convenience.

If you decide not to sign and return the waiver, the law requires that after 90 days from the date of mailing this letter (150 days if this letter is addressed to you outside the United States) we assess and bill you for the deficiencies. However, if within the time stated you contest this determination by filing a petition with the United States Tax Court, Box 70, Washington, D.C. 20044, we may not assess any deficiencies and bill you until after the Tax Court has decided your case. You can obtain a copy of the rules for filing a petition by writing to the Clerk of the Tax Court at the Court's Washington, D.C. address stated above.

If you intend to file a petition with the United States Tax Court, you must do so within the time stated above (90 or 150 days, as the case may be); this period is fixed by law, and the Court cannot consider your case if your petition is filed late.

If you have any questions, please contact the person whose name and telephone number are shown above.

Sincerely yours,
Donald C. Alexander
Commissioner
By

Enclosures:
Statement
Waiver, Form 870
Envelope

District Director

EXHIBIT A

Form L-21 (Rev. 2-74)

After receiving this STATUTORY NOTICE OF DEFICIENCY, the taxpayer will normally take affirmative action by filing a protest in the form of a PETITION to the United States Tax Court. Directions for preparing this are found in Rules 20 to 25 inclusive of TITLE III in the *Rules of Practice and Procedure*. These deal with the commencement of the Petitioner's Case, the Filing of Documents, their form and style. The filing fee is $10.00; all papers must be given to, and served by, the Clerk of the Court. Proper captions must be placed on all papers; the signature of the Petitioner or his counsel and its date shall be included in all documents.

There shall be four confirmed copies of each document, together with the signed original — see Rule 91(b). Typewritten papers shall be double-spaced, typed on one side only, and shall be on plain white paper 8½ x 11 inches, not less than sixteen pounds to the ream, except copies. Printed papers shall be 10- or 12-point type. All papers, typed or printed, shall have an inside margin not less than 1¼ inches wide, bound on left side only, and, except briefs, have no backs or covers. All citations shall be underscored in the text when typed and in italics when printed.

Since the Court may be very particular, it may reject a petition unless these formal requirements are strictly observed.

The APPEAL and PETITION may be filed by the taxpayer himself, or through counsel. The reader will note that the PETITION does not cite court decisions or marshall supporting evidence. It simply recites certain facts and challenges the allegations of the IRS on each issue or item to be tested in a court trial and in subsequent briefs.

On the following pages, we reproduce a PETITION and REQUEST FOR PLACE OF TRIAL just as they were submitted in reply to the NOTICE OF DEFICIENCY reproduced on the previous page.

B. HOW THE CASE OF THE ASSOCIATION WAS SETTLED

There can be little doubt that the purpose of the IRS in regard to the Association for Political Freedom was its suppression as a voice of dissent, rather than any expectation of collecting

PETITION

UNITED STATES TAX COURT

Association for Political Freedom)
    Petitioner   )
)
   v.   )   DOCKET NO. 0000-00
)
Commissioner of Internal Revenue)
    Respondent)

PETITION

The Petitioner hereby petitions for a redetermination of the deficiencies set forth by the Commissioner of Internal Revenue in his NOTICE OF DEFICIENCY Symbols: Code 000: 000: 0000: 000, dated February 00, 19__, and, as the basis for his case, alleges as follows:

1. The Petitioner is a Corporation with its principal office at 10,000 Anystreet, Anytown, California, 90000. Forms 990, Return of Organization Exempt from Income Tax, for the periods here involved, were filed with the Office of Internal Revenue Service, Ogden, Utah.

2. The NOTICE OF DEFICIENCY (a copy of which is attached and marked Exhibit A) was mailed to the Petitioner on February 00, 19__, and was issued by the Office of Internal Revenue Service at Los Angeles, California.

3. The deficiencies as determined by the Commissioner are in income taxes under Section 11 of the 1954 Internal Revenue Code and penalties under Section 6651(a) of the 1954 Internal Revenue Code as follows, all of which are in dispute: (here follows a recap of the deficiencies and penalties set forth in the NOTICE OF DEFICIENCY).

4. The determination of tax set forth in said NOTICE OF DEFICIENCY is based upon the following errors:

(a) The Commissioner erroneously determined that Petitioner does not qualify as an organization which is exempt from taxation under section 501 of the Internal Revenue Code.

(b) The Commissioner erroneously increased gross receipts in the amount of $0,000.00 for the year ended April 30, 1969.

(c) The Commissioner erroneously disallowed deductions for distribution and promotion in the amounts of $0,000.00, $0,000.00, and $0,000.00 for the years ended April 30, 1969, April 30, 1970, and April 30, 1971, respectively.

(d) The Commissioner erroneously determined penalties under section 6651(a) of the 1954 Internal Revenue Code for each of the years ended April 30, 1969, April 30, 1970, and April 30, 1971.

5. The facts upon which the Petitioner relies, as the basis for its case, are as follows:

(a) (1) Petitioner was organized as a tax-exempt organization and its charter was filed with the Secretary of State. of _____ on April CO, 19__. (Its purposes as stated in its charter are here given in detail.)

(2) Petitioner has no stock and no members; is managed by its officers, Executive Committee and Board of Directors; no Officer or Director receives any salary or other emolument ; no one profits from its activities in any way.

(3) (The goals and purposes of the Corporation are here restated.)

(4) The publications of the Corporation are sold and distributed without profit to any individual or even to the Corporation.

(5) The officers of the Corporation receive no pay or other compensation except minimum salaries for work actually performed at its principal office.

(6) Petitioner was not organized for profit, but has operated since its inception and continues to operate exclusively for the promotion of social welfare. It was run in this manner from its beginning and is still so operated, as shown by its financial records and its publications.

(b) (Here is a statement that one of the adjustments made by the Commissioner is erroneous, giving the exact amount of the error.

(c) (Here is a statement that another adjustment of the Commissioner is in error, giving the exact amount and nature of the error.)

(d) (Here is a statement challenging another adjustment made by the Commissioner and stating the amount of the error.)

(e) (Here is still another and similar correction of error.)

(f) Petitioner declares that $00,000.00, $00,000.00, and $00,000.00, deducted for distribution and promotion for the years ended April 30, 1969, April 30, 1970, and April 30, 1971, respectively, represent items of many kinds and the Petitioner does not know what the specific items are which have been disallowed in the amounts of $0,000.00, $0,000.00, and $0,000.00, for the years shown above respectively, but Petitioner believes that all such sums are deductible as ordinary business expenses.

(g) Petitioner disputes the method by which Commissioner arrived at a tax-computation based on inventory.

(h) Petitioner filed Form 990 for the years ending April 30, 1969, April 30, 1970, and April 30, 1971. Because of this fact, Petitioner has not been required to file Form 1120, U.S. Corporation Income Tax Return for the periods involved.

(i) (Petitioner here explains that because subscriptions do not expire until some time after the close of each fiscal year, prepayments in various amounts of cash ranging from $00,000 to $00,000 would not be taxable in the years received even if the Corporation were one organized and operating for profit.)

Wherefore Petitioner qualifies as an organization which is exempt from taxation under section 501 of the Internal Revenue Code and prays that this Court hear this case and determine:

(1) That it does so qualify for exemption and

(2) That there is no deficiency in the income tax or penalty under Code sections 6651(a) for the years ended April 30, 1969, April 30, 1970, and April 30, 1971 nor under section 11 of the same for the same years.

DATED: Month, Day, Year   (Signed)

GOODMAN COUNSELLOR
Counsel for Petitioner
Telephone Number
Address and Area Code

UNITED STATES TAX COURT

Association for Political Freedom	)	
Petitioner	)	
	)	
v.	)	DOCKET NO. C000-00
	)	
Commissioner of Internal Revenue	)	
Respondent	)	

REQUEST FOR PLACE OF TRIAL

Petitioner hereby requests that trial in this case be held at

Los Angeles, California
(City and State)

Goodman Counsellor
GOODMAN COUNSELLOR

Counsel for Petitioner
Address
Telephone Number

DATED: Month, Day, Year

U. S. TAX COURT
GRANTED
Date

PETITION SERVED ON RESPONDENT   Date
FILING FEE ALSO ACKNOWLEDGED

taxes. There was no conceivable legal basis on which to base an assessment; nor had the Association been guilty of anything which could justify the revocation of its exemption as a 501(c)(4) organization.

After the above PETITION was filed, the IRS finally released the Bill of Particulars which it had withheld for several years and which listed its disallowances. However, these were so unfounded that the IRS case for tax-assessments collapsed. The Agency then offered a compromise: if the Association would agree to its loss of exempt status, no demand would be made for money. However, when this was rejected, the IRS permitted the exemption to stand; but did so only one week before the case was scheduled for trial.

And so after its long siege of harassment and the expenditure of nearly $15,000 by the Association to prove its innocence, the IRS finally admitted that it had been completely wrong from the start and that no action of any kind should ever have been initiated against it.

However, had the officers of the Association known how to defend themselves, they could have forced the IRS to divulge its Bill of Particulars at the beginning, to discuss each and every disallowance at that time, and thus avoid the misery and expense which seriously crippled its activities and almost caused its bankruptcy. Actually, the one to blame was a lawyer who had been given power of attorney and who, without counsulting the editors, wrote a letter to the IRS waiving the exempt status of the organization, an action which led to all the troubles which followed.

C. THE TRIAL AND THE SUBSEQUENT BRIEFS

The filing of the PETITION represents only the first step in Tax Court litigation. To this, the Commissioner has sixty days to prepare his ANSWER in which he must state whether he concedes any of the positions taken by the Petitioner and advise the latter and the Court fully of the nature of his defense. It must contain a specific denial or admission of each allegation made by the Petitioner, who then has forty-five days to file a REPLY or REBUTTAL if he chooses to do so; however, this is not

mandatory for, in the absence of a REPLY, the affirmative
allegations of the Commissioner in his ANSWER "will be deemed
denied unless the Commissioner within forty-five days ... files a
motion for an order that specified allegations in the ANSWER
shall be deemed admitted."

To all these written pleadings — which precede the trial —
amendments may be filed, depositions taken, and supplemental
pleadings made; or the dispute may be settled at any time by
negotiation and agreement. If a trial is to occur, the date will be
set by the Court.

At the trial, the adversaries will present oral arguments
explaining their positions in detail and citing the authorities on
which they rely for favorable determinations. Within sixty days
after the conclusion of the trial, "unless otherwise directed,"

> Each party shall file his initial brief, including his proposed
> findings of fact and legal argument ... A party thereafter
> deciding to file a responsive brief shall do so, including ob-
> jections to proposed findings of fact, within 30 days after the
> expiration of the period for filing the initial brief...

Rule 151 provides that all briefs must be filed in duplicate
together with an additional copy for each person to be served. All
briefs must include:

(1) Following the title page, a table of contents, with page
references, followed by a list of legal citations arranged alpha-
betically, stating the pages in the brief on which they are cited.
Citations given in the text are to be underscored or in italics.

(2) A statement of the nature of the controversy, the tax
involved, and the issues to be decided.

(3) Proposed findings of fact based on the evidence, in the
form of numbered statements, each of which shall be complete
and consist of a concise statement of essential fact and not a
recital of testimony or argument. In an Answering or Reply Brief,
the party shall set forth his objections, with reasons therefor, to
any proposed finding by the other party; he may also set forth
alternative findings of fact.

(4) A concise statement of the facts on which the party
relies.

(5) The Argument, which sets forth and discusses the points of law involved and any disputed questions of fact.

(6) The signature of counsel or the party submitting the brief shall be included, as in the PETITION above shown.

After receiving and considering the arguments presented at the trial and the contents of the briefs, the Tax Court will render its detailed decision. All this is an elaborate procedure, more or less time-consuming depending on the nature of the dispute.

D.   THE BATTLE OF PHIL AND SUE LONG

The dispute of Phil and Sue Long of Bellevue, Washington, followed an IRS determination that two real-estate corporations, of which Mr. Long was president, had become personal holding companies after they sold their assets and were therefore subject to a 70 per cent tax on virtually all income not distributed in the form of dividends. The IRS declared that he was entitled to no more compensation than $1.00 per month for each installment the Corporations received on outstanding contracts, thus reducing his compensation from $600 to $150 a month.

After the IRS audited the returns of the corporations, these were assessed taxes totalling $38,144 for the years 1966, 1967, and 1968, in addition to the $21,442 which had already been paid. Although the IRS dropped all but five of the thirty-three claims originally made, it was still demanding $42,000, including interest, late in 1972. In the meantime, Mr. Long had published a series of articles in the Washington *Post* describing life in America under the IRS; and, as noted, he was the man who took the Service to court and forced it to surrender the material published by the Church of Scientology. He stated that, in his opinion, the only reason the IRS refrained from invoking the Jeopardy Assessment against him was the fact that, as a result of his publicity and activity, he had become a highly "sensitive case."

E.   THE FINAL OUTCOME OF THE LONG LITIGATION

In 1973, the Tax Court found in favor of the IRS and upheld its contention that (1) the Petitioners were personal holding companies subject to the tax imposed by Section 541 of the Code; and (2) that Mr. Long was not entitled to more than $150 a month for the services he rendered to the Petitioners.

The wheels of justice grind slowly; and it was not until four years later that the Long-appeal was adjudicated in a higher court. Under date of March 28, 1977, Mr. Long wrote: "... during the last seven years, we have researched into the IRS much deeper than most taxpayers and have found out a lot ... Because of this experience, we have found where the IRS is powerful and also where it is weak ... the IRS system and the judicial system have evolved into contests much more influenced by 'skills' than by 'what is right.'

"So our successes with the IRS are not because we are 'right,' but more because we have 'done our home work.'

"On March 10, we were in the U.S. Court of Appeals in San Francisco and we went *Pro Se* ... the brief and the reply were written by Sue and she did the 30 minute Oral Argument ... The questions by the judges and the review of all factors make us feel that we have a good chance to win ...

"We hope to win. It will be good for all taxpayers if we win. The taxpayer who loses in court loses not only for himself, but in the area of case law which will make it harder for others in the future to take their cases to court ..."

The hopes of the Longs were fulfilled; for on December 2, 1977, the Court of Appeals reversed the Tax Court and ruled in favor of the Longs: they did not have to pay one penny of the huge assessment which would otherwise have been collected from them and which would probably have left them virtually destitute; for, in addition to the original levy, there would have been heavy charges for interest and other fees. Instead, they finally received refunds totalling $1,657.83.

F.   THE BRIEF FILED BY THE LONGS IN THE TAX COURT

The 150-page brief which Mr. Long filed has been praised as a model of pleading by both lawyers and laymen. For the benefit of taxpayers who wish to appear *pro se* in the Tax Court, we therefore reproduce some of the pages of this brief, which include

the following:
  (1) The first title page
  (2) The entire TABLE OF CONTENTS
  (3) Three of the eight pages comprising the list of 115 court cases cited
  (4) The second title page
  (5) Four pages of the portion stating the Nature of the Tax in controversy
  (6) The first two pages under ARGUMENT, dealing with ISSUE ONE
  (7) The SUMMARY OF ISSUE ONE
  (8) The first three pages under ARGUMENT dealing with ISSUE TWO
  (9) The concluding three pages under ISSUE TWO and the SUMMARY of this ISSUE
  (10) The CONCLUSION
All this material is so clear and so complete that the *pro-se* litigant should be able to prepare a similar brief, at least insofar as the format is concerned, on the basis of his own research, and with little or no professional help.

THE   UNITED   STATES   TAX   COURT

Docket Nos. 2885-71, 2886-71

PARKSIDE, INC., Petitioner

v.

COMMISSIONER OF INTERNAL REVENUE, Respondent

BEACONCREST, INC., Petitioner

v.

COMMISSIONER OF INTERNAL REVENUE, Respondent

BRIEF FOR PETITIONERS

Philip H. Long, President
PARKSIDE, INC.
BEACONCREST, INC.
P. O. Box 595
Bellevue, Washington 98009

TABLE OF CONTENTS

LIST OF CITATIONS

THE UNITED STATES TAX COURT

———

Docket Nos. 2885-71, 2886-71

———

PARKSIDE, INC., Petitioner

v.

COMMISSIONER OF INTERNAL REVENUE, Respondent

BEACONCREST, INC., Petitioner

v.

COMMISSIONER OF INTERNAL REVENUE, Respondent

———

BRIEF FOR PETITIONERS

———

Petitioners seek a judgment in their favor that no deficiencies in taxes are due from them. The above entitled cases, having been consolidated for purposes of trial, briefing and opinion, came on for hearing before the Honorable Cynthia H. Hall, Judge, on Thursday, May 24, 1973 in Washington, D.C.

Simultaneous briefs are to be filed.by July 25, 1973 and
reply briefs by August 24, 1973.

NATURE OF THE TAX IN CONTROVERSY

The Commissioner of Internal Revenue determined the following deficiencies in income and personal holding company taxes
for the calendar years 1966, 1967 and 1968 in the case of
petitioner, Parkside, Inc., and for the calendar years 1967 and
1968 for petitioner, Beaconcrest, Inc.:

		PARKSIDE, INC. (Docket No. 2885-71)	BEACONCREST, INC. (Docket No. 2886-71)
1966		$ 3,975.25	---
1967		10,615.65	$ 9,260.77
1968		8,593.45	8,806.60
	TOTAL	$23,184.35	$18,067.37

totaling for both cases $41,251.72.

The proposed income tax deficiencies in dispute in these
two cases arise from:

> (a) the imposition of the personal holding
>   company tax on the petitioners for the
>   years here involved,
>
> (b) the disallowance as unreasonable
>   compensation of all but $150 a month of
>   the $600 a month paid by Beaconcrest,
>   Inc. to its president, Philip H. Long
>   for the years in issue

(Respondent has conceded the remaining adjustments in dispute
involving the disallowance of various business expenses and an
investment credit reported on petitioners' returns.)

ISSUES PRESENTED FOR DECISION[1]

(1) Were the petitioners in the years here involved
personal holding companies and subject to the
imposition of personal holding company taxes?

(2) Was the compensation paid in the years 1967 and
1968 to Philip H. Long reasonable in amount?

STATEMENT OF FACTS

Some of the facts in this case have been previously
stipulated and are contained in the May 22, 1973,Stipulation
and May 23, 1973 Supplemental Stipulation filed with the Court
and hereafter designated by S-(paragraph number). Other
evidence was presented at trial, hereafter designated T(page
number):(line number) from the transcript of the proceedings.
The facts are set forth below:

---

[1]In the petitions originally filed with this Court and in
the trial memorandum filed on or before May 7, 1973, petitioners
in addition to the two issues raised above (and those which
respondent has now conceded) raised certain constitutional
issues regarding denial of due process and equal protection of
the laws under the Fifth, Fourteenth and Sixteenth Amendments
to the Constitution and the denial of First Amendment rights
under the Constitution. On May 22, 1973 the Court in granting
the respondent's motion to quash eight subpoenas duces tecum
served by petitioners upon certain Internal Revenue Service
officials, in effect, ruled upon these constitutional questions
in ruling that the questions raised and documentary and
testimonial information sought were irrelevant to the
controversy before the Court and by precluding petitioners from
introducing at trial necessary evidence on these matters.

1. The petitioners, Parkside, Inc. and Beaconcrest, Inc.,
are corporations organized and existing under the corporate laws
of the state of Washington. (S-1)

2. Parkside, Inc. and Beaconcrest, Inc., both cash basis,
calendar year taxpayers, filed their federal income tax returns
for the period here involved with the District Director of
Internal Revenue, Tacoma, Washington for the years 1966 and 1967,
and with the Director, Internal Revenue Service Center, Ogden,
Utah for the year 1968. Petitioners filed amended returns
for the years here involved with the Director, Internal Revenue
Service Center, Ogden, Utah. (S-2,3)

3. Since 1960 the stock in the two corporations has been
owned by the following brothers and sister (hereafter referred
to as "shareholders"):

> Philip H. Long
> James Robert Long
> Dwight Stanley Long
> Erna (Long) McKenzie

who each hold an undivided quarter interest in the two corporations
The stock in Parkside, Inc. passed to the shareholders in 1960
upon the death of their father, an individual active in the
real estate business in Seattle both individually and through
corporations as an operative builder constructing buildings
for sale and/or rental. Beaconcrest, Inc. was formed by the
shareholders on August 1, 1960, after the death of their father,
to receive part of the assets of another corporation, Standard
Homes, Inc., organized by their father to construct buildings

for sale and/or rental. Beaconcrest was formed to rent and
sell those properties. (S-4;T122:19-20)

4. The principal assets of Parkside, Inc. at the time
the stock passed to the shareholders consisted of 26 duplexes
(52 units) originally built by Parkside, and located as a unit
in the Holman Road area of Seattle. The principal assets of
Beaconcrest, Inc. at the time of incorporation consisted of
21 duplexes (42 units) originally built by Standard Homes,
and located as a unit in the Beacon Hill area in the southern
part of Seattle. (S-5)

5. Since the shareholders' father came to Seattle in
1907 he had run various building businesses, in selling of
property over the years. (T17:8-10)

6. The shareholders' father started building duplexes
for the first time in about 1942. During the war years he
built about 20 duplexes. During the war builders could only
sell half the duplexes they built. He was therefore forced to
hold a number of duplexes and at the end of the war he had an
inventory of about 10 duplexes. At that point he was fortunate
enough to sell those over a short period of time. (T18:9-17)

7. After the war the shareholders' father continued to
build duplexes. Parkside, Inc. and Standard Homes, Inc. were
corporations formed and used by him for building, renting and
selling duplexes. (S-4,T18:7-9;121:9-24;122:7-10)

8. In 1945 or 1946 the shareholders' father was probably in his most favorable financial position over his lifetime. He had through the sale of duplexes after the war accumulated $30,000 or $40,000 in cash, had about $20,000 in equity in duplexes he hadn't sold, and obligations of approximately $100,000 in mortgages. In contrast, by August of 1959 when he died he had accumulated total obligations for mortgages alone of $550,000 and had other obligations totaling between $100,000 and $200,000. (T18:18-25;19:1)

9. In August of 1959 the monthly obligations which the shareholders inherited were in the vicinity of $8,000 a month while the income from rent without any sales was less than that amount. (T18:4-7)

10. Parkside, Inc. as of the beginning of 1960 had a surplus account which showed a deficit balance of $-15,732.90 from prior years' losses. Its initial capitalization of $12,750 was very small. (Ex 1-A)

11. Duplexes are a very unique business in Seattle and a very difficult one from both a sales and rental perspective. Aside from the shareholders' father, perhaps only six other individuals in the last 30 years owned as many as 20 duplexes. Three of those had gone bankrupt and the other three got out of the business. (T40:24-25;76:11-25;77:1-6;120:20-25;121:1-5)

12. In January of 1960 Philip H. Long left his former employment at Northwestern Mutual Insurance Company to assume the task of running the two corporations for the shareholders,

ARGUMENT

ISSUE ONE: PERSONAL HOLDING COMPANY TAX

The first issue before the Court is the Commissioner's
imposition of the personal holding company tax on the petitioners:

   (i) for the years 1966, 1967 and 1968 in the
       case of Parkside, Inc.

   (ii) for the years 1967 and 1968 in the case
       of Beaconcrest, Inc.

Petitioners contend they are not and were not personal
holding companies and were not therefore subject to the imposition
of the personal holding company tax. The dispute in these cases
arise over whether petitioners met the adjusted ordinary gross
income test.[1] This dispute in turn rests upon a subsidiary
question which is the material issue in dispute, namely:

> whether 47 duplexes sold by petitioners were held
> primarily for sale to customers in the ordinary
> course of their trade or business

During the years in issue the petitioners received income
designated as interest on their federal income tax returns from
real estate contracts for these duplexes sold by them during the
years 1965 and 1966. Petitioners contend that under section
543(b)(3) of the Code, this interest for purposes of determining
personal holding company status is classified as "rents" and
is not personal holding company income.[2] The Commissioner

---

[1]It has been stipulated that the stock was owned equally
by four shareholders; thus, there is no dispute over the stock
ownership test.

[2]The Commissioner does not dispute the fact that should
interest be classified as rents it is not personal holding
company income to the petitioners.

disputes this contention. The Commissioner does, however, concede
that aside from this one issue the petitioners have never received
any personal holding company income from any other source in the
years in issue or during any prior years. (Stipulation, para. 16)

Under section 543(b)(3) of the Internal Revenue Code, rent
is defined as follows:

> ...the term "rents" means compensation, however
> designated for the use of, or right to use,
> property, and the interest on debts owed to the
> corporation, to the extent such debts represent
> the price for which real property held primarily
> for sale to customers in the ordinary course of
> its trade or business was sold or exchanged by
> the corporation. (emphasis supplied)

I. OVERVIEW

Before turning to petitioners' arguments in detail, their
essential points will be briefly summarized here:

First, we are here dealing with a severe penalty, the
imposition of which on petitioners was never the end result
sought by Congress. Petitioners have never received personal
holding company income and in no way resemble an "incorporated
pocketbook". Petitioners are clearly bonafide family real

One by one the methods employed for merchandising these
duplexes carrying out petitioners' "profit motive" --
individual sales, aggressive sales promotion and solicitation,
hard and extended price negotiations, contract sales, low down
payments, low monthly payments fixed for the long terms of
these contracts, payment of real estate taxes and other costs,
property condition guarantees, assistance in starting up a
duplex business -- add up to what cannot be denied as
substantially larger prices at sale. The low downpayments
alone were estimated to increase the price received by $1000
to $2000 or upwards of $80,000 on total sales prices.

To tax this value received as a result of petitioners'
direct efforts in sales merchandising as a capital gain would
be to apply the provisions of the taxing statute so broadly as
to defeat rather than further congressional purposes.

VII. SUMMARY

An examination from every perspective -- from the will of
Congress, the statutory language, the narrow construction
required of such a harsh and double exception to normal tax
requirements, the complete absence over a 40-year period of
any case law supportive of the government's claims, and the
very facts themselves -- clearly document that petitioners are
not and never have been personal holding companies. Unquestionably,
petitioners held these duplexes primarily for sale to customers
in the ordinary course of their trade or business.

ISSUE TWO: REASONABLE COMPENSATION

    The second issue presented for decison concerns the question
of reasonable compensation of Philip Long for services he
rendered Beaconcrest, Inc. as its president. The years involved
in this issue are 1967 and 1968. During those calendar years
Philip Long as president of Beaconcrest, Inc. received a total
of the following:

1967	$7,300
1968	7,200

which was paid at the rate of $600 a month.

    According to Section 162(a) of the Internal Revenue Code,
a corporation "shall be allowed as a deduction* * *a reasonable
allowance for salaries or other compensation for personal
services actually rendered." The Commissioner, however, allowed
as a deduction only $150 a month or a total of $1800 in each
of the two years.

    Petitioner Beaconcrest's position is twofold: First, it
is its position that the payments it made to Philip Long were
entirely reasonable in amount solely in light of the services
actually rendered and provided by Mr. Long to it during 1967
and 1968. Second, it is alternatively or supplementally
contended that such payments were wholly reasonable in light
of past services performed by Philip Long for Beaconcrest, Inc.
for which services Mr. Long was grossly undercompensated in
prior years.

    Courts have evolved many factors to consider on this
question. Mayson Manufacturing Company v. Commissioner (6th
Cir., 1949), 178 F.2d 115,119; King Quirk & Co., Inc., TC Memo
1961-274, 20 T.C.M. 1429, 1434. Reasonable compensation is a
question of fact, necessarily turning upon the particular facts
and circumstances of each case. R. J. Nicoll Company (1972),
59 T.C. 37,48; S & B Realty Company (1970), 54 T.C. 863,872.

In laying the foundation for later discussion there are
several factors which can be dispensed with rather quickly.
First, it is clear that we are not here dealing with a question
involving a large or exorbitant salary. It is a far cry from
the situation in the original landmark case in this area,
Botany Worsted Mills v. United States (1929), 278 U.S. 282,293,
involving a one-year bonus payment of $1,565,739.39 paid ten
company directors in addition to their regular salaries where
the Court noted:

> * * *it is clear that extraordinary, unusual and
> extravagent amounts paid by a corporation to its
> officers in the guise and form of compensation
> for their services, but having no substantial
> relation to the measure of their services and being
> utterly disproportioned to their value, are not
> in reality payment for services, and cannot be
> regarded as "ordinary and necessary expenses"
> within the meaning of the section* * *

Clearly the salary received by Mr. Long can hardly be
described as "extravagant," particularly in view of the fact
that during this period he held no outside remunerative
employment, and for his salary of $600 a month was available
to the corporation on a full-time basis, giving his undivided
attention to the task. As a matter of fact, Beaconcrest could
not have hired the lowest unskilled laborer for the salary
it paid Mr. Long during those years. (Stipulation, para. 20)

In limiting compensation where it is "extravagant" in
amount and "utterly disproportioned" to the value of services
rendered, neither Congress nor the courts had any intention
of denying to small family businesses the right to pay a
living wage to their sole operating officer on whose shoulders
the success or failure of the business rests.

Nor do we believe there is any dispute that Mr. Long is
a valuable and skilled executive who would be paid a great deal
more elsewhere than he received as president of Beaconcrest
during 1967 and 1968. These were in fact what would usually be
described as his peak earning capacity years. Mr. Long neither

sought nor wanted this position. It is clear he would have
very much preferred other employment during this period,
accepting this job at great personal financial sacrifice only
out of a sense of family responsibility.

Where then does the dispute lie? As far as petitioner can
ascertain, the Commissioner's disallowance is based upon the
twin findings that beyond extremely minor clerical duties,
Mr. Long performed no services for Beaconcrest during 1967
and 1968 (T15:11-13) and that prior years' services rendered
Beaconcrest were already adequately compensated for since:
"Similar salaries had been paid by Beaconcrest to Philip Long
since its inception." (respondent's trial memorandum, page 3,
lines 3-4).[24]

On neither point do the facts sustain the Commissioner's
findings.

I. OVERVIEW.

Did Mr. Long render important and continuing services
to Beaconcrest during 1967 and 1968? Unquestionably the
answer is yes.

As chief executive during the critical 1967-68 period
immediately following sales, his services were especially
valuable. He identified risks faced by the company, the steps
necessary for the company to best minimize the impact on the
financial fortunes of the company such risks posed, and was
available as well as called upon to make decisions concerning

---

[24]The Commissioner's own findings indicate Mr. Long was
grossly undercompensated. In basing their determination upon
a valuation of Mr. Long's past services to Beaconcrest at no
less than $7200-7300 a year, the government concedes that such
services were worth at least $50,400-$51,000 (7×$7200-7300),
in contrast to the total amount Beaconcrest paid him of only
$22,775 during 1960-1966. (Even including payments received
from Parkside for services he separately rendered it, Mr. Long's
total compensation from all sources during 1960-66 was almost
$10,000 less than the government's allowance of $7200-7300 a
year solely for Beaconcrest services.)

Further, through Mr. Long's direct and supervisory efforts as operating manager the merchandising strategy was successfully executed. Due to these direct efforts and the inducements he devised, much larger prices were obtained. Equally importantly, through his careful selection of buyers, as the future itself revealed, foreclosure problems for the company were avoided.

The Beaconcrest duplexes were sold for a total sales price of $355,365.00. The amount Beaconcrest paid just the real estate salesmen amounted to $21,321.90. Surely, in light of the fact that it was Mr. Long's original and careful decisions and his ability to successfully effectuate those decisions that were responsible for these results, his services could hardly be valued at less than what was paid the salesmen acting under his direction.

From June 1964 on, Mr. Long also assumed the additional duty of keeping all the corporate books and records for which an unrelated party had been compensated at the rate of $200 a month.[37] Further, Mr. Long from mid-1964 on provided a separate building rent-free for Beaconcrest's offices. For comparable square footage, its previous office space rental had run $144 a month. While it shared this office space with Parkside, Inc., the amount of office space it alone would have needed would not have been materially less. In evaluating how much Beaconcrest would have had to pay to rent office space it alone needed, it is clear that the $144 charge would not have been materially reduced. Thus the office space furnished by Mr. Long for the period of mid-1964 through 1968 would have cost Beaconcrest

---

[37]Such compensation did, however, include payment for keeping Parkside's books as well. While Mr. Long assumed the task for both companies we are not here concerned with the equally apparent gross inadequacies in the compensation Mr. Long received from Parkside for services he separately rendered to it over the years.

approximately $7,766, not including any allowance for rising
rent levels. If the value of his bookkeeping services for
just mid-1964 through 1966 at the conservative rate of $100 a
month were added to this amount, together the total for these
minor services is the equivalent of the total amount disallowed
by the Commissioner. If Mr. Long was undercompensated for
his services as bookkeeper and provider of office space, surely
there can be little doubt that as chief executive and operating
manager his services were grossly undercompensated.

From whatever perspective or period focused upon, the
evidence on obvious undercompensation cannot be disputed. Mr.
Long was not adequately compensated in any one of the prior
seven years, and during three of those years he was not
compensated at all beyond a token payment of $375. The value
of the many and extensive services he ably performed during
those years for which he was inadequately compensated many
times exceed the amount disallowed by the Commissioner.

The benefits received by Beaconcrest for Mr. Long's
services and his foregoing of adequate compensation during
this period were of critical importance. Mr. Long testified,
and the facts amply document his testimony, that he kept his
salary as minimal as possible (just to cover his living
expenses) in order to conserve Beaconcrest's limited cash
during difficult and trying times. His undercompensated
services were easily THE factor that kept the corporation from
bankruptcy, and the business judgments he made and carried
out allowed the corporation to pay off a major portion of the
debts accumulated by the shareholders' father and still provide
promise of return.

Further it was established that the shareholders expected
to make up this difference to Mr. Long when the company was
financially able. The other three shareholders, in fact,
repeatedly urged Mr. Long to more adequately compensate himself
in those years and they relented only in the face of his
insistance that the cash just wasn't available and with the

further general understanding that eventually when the corporation was able they would "settle up" so that he got his fair share out of it for services he had performed over the years.

The compensation received in 1967 and 1968 by Philip Long from Beaconcrest, Inc. can fairly be described as payments for services performed in the past as well as payment for services performed during 1967 and 1968. Philip Long's services to Beaconcrest during prior years were grossly undercompensated. Since amounts deductible are not limited to services rendered in current years, the compensation received during 1967 and 1968 was wholly reasonable in light of these undercompensated past services.

X. SUMMARY

Compensation paid to Philip Long by Beaconcrest, Inc. was entirely reasonable in amount solely in light of the services actually rendered by Mr. Long to it during 1967 and 1968. Further, such compensation was wholly reasonable in light of past services performed by Philip Long for Beaconcrest, Inc. for which services Mr. Long was grossly undercompensated in prior years.

CONCLUSION

On both issues petitioners should be sustained. Unquestionably they are not and never have been personal holding companies and the compensation paid by Beaconcrest, Inc. to its president, Philip Long, was completely reasonable in amount.

Respectfully submitted,

Philip H. Long, President
PARKSIDE, INC.
BEACONCREST, INC.
P. O. BOX 595
Bellevue, Washington 98009

Ten   Going to the Circuit Court of Appeals

A.   *THE BATTLE OF DR. EDWARD A. CUPP*

Dr. E. A. Cupp, a chiropractor of Hopwood, Pennsylvania, has been fighting the IRS for years, challenging it especially on the monetary issue and its authority to collect taxes by the methods it uses. After doing a vast amount of research in regard to the doctor — who had not paid any taxes for years — it decided to bring a civil instead of a criminal action against him by reconstructing the income from his medical practice. Thus it was that he was able to appeal to the Tax Court and then to the United States District Court of Appeals. The former rendered its decision against him in a 37-page document filed on February 14, 1975. This Opinion consists, first, of the Findings or Decisions of the Court, under the caption HELD:, which has five subheadings covering four pages; second, FINDINGS OF FACT, covering twelve, in which a minute history of the case is given; and, third, OPINION, covering twenty-one pages, in which 48 court cases are cited and/or quoted.

There is no doubt that the government spent hundreds or perhaps thousands of man-hours in its battle with Dr. Cupp over a period of more than seven years. Interestingly enough, the adverse Opinion handed down by the Court contains a statement which, if sustained, would invalidate the monetary system of the United States. In rejecting Dr. Cupp's contention that only gold and silver constitute lawful money, the Court declared that ARTICLE I, Section 1, of the Constitution applies only to the states and not to the national government. However, this statement opens a Pandora's box of possibilities: if it really *does* apply to the states, then all checks paid out by them must be redeemable in gold or silver; and, since no state can issue money and since two kinds of national currency do not and cannot exist, it follows that the Federal government would also be forced to adopt a specie standard. So far as we know, this is the first time that any United States court of record has touched upon this sensitive issue.

Since Dr. Cupp disagreed with the findings of the Tax Court, he posted bond in order to stay execution of its decision and, within the thirty-day limit permitted, filed a brief in the United States Court of Appeals for the Third Circuit, in which he pointed out the weaknesses and contradictions of the determinations made in the Tax Court and in which he presented new arguments and additional court opinions and citations in support of his position. Whenever such a document is submitted, the Clerk of the Tax Court forwards it to the Clerk of that Court of Appeals which is to receive it and hear the case. A complete record of the dispute will then be sent to both parties involved in litigation together with an index of the record on appeal.

On April 27, 1976, seven years after the doctor filed his first "improper" return — which included no payment — the Tax Court entered its Final Decision, which we reproduce on the next page. This, however, was only the signal for a new phase of his battle; for shortly thereafter, he filed a 37-page brief in the Third Circuit Court of Appeals, portions of which we reproduce. The format in which this is written can be used as a model for any similar appeal.

Within ninety days after the Tax Court renders its Opinion and Decision or Final Determination, either party may appeal to the nearest United States District Court of Appeals by filling out and submitting the following form to the Clerk of the Tax Court:

NOTICE OF APPEAL TO THE COURT OF APPEALS
UNITED STATES TAX COURT

John Q. Taxpayer)
      Petitioner)
)
       v.)   DOCKET NO.
)
Commissioner of Internal Revenue)
      Respondent)

NOTICE OF APPEAL

Notice is hereby given that _____ hereby appeals to the United States Court of Appeals for _____ Circuit (that part of) the decision of this Court entered in the above-captioned proceeding on the _____ day of _____, 19 ____ (relating to _____).

_____
Party or Counsel

_____
Post Office Address

UNITED STATES TAX COURT
WASHINGTON

EDWARD A. CUPP,
                Petitioner,

         v.

COMMISSIONER OF INTERNAL REVENUE,
               Respondent.

Docket No. 4828-73.

DECISION

Pursuant to the determination of the Court as set forth in its Opinion filed October 14, 1975, respondent filed a computation for entry of decision on December 12, 1975. Thereafter, petitioner filed a computation and respondent filed objections thereto. Pursuant to prior notice to the parties, these computations were called for hearing on the Motions Session of the Court on April 7, 1976, at which time petitioner appeared on his own behalf and respondent was represented by counsel. After due consideration, the facts recited in respondent's computation are incorporated herein as the findings of the Court, and it is

ORDERED and DECIDED: That there are deficiencies in income taxes due from the petitioner for the taxable years 1969, 1970 and 1971 in the amounts of $7,878.70, $13,276.77 and $14,361.09, respectively;

That there are additions to the tax due from the petitioner for the taxable years 1969, 1970 and 1971, under the provisions of section 6651(a), I.R.C. 1954, in the amounts of $1,969.68, $3,319.19 and $3,590.27, respectively; and

That there are additions to the tax due from the petitioner for the taxable years 1969, 1970 and 1971, under the provisions of section 6653(a), I.R.C. 1954, in the amounts of $543.93, $663.84 and $718.05, respectively.

(Signed) Irene F. Scott

Judge.

Entered: APR 27 1976

B. BRIEF FILED BY DR. CUPP IN THE COURT OF APPEALS

IN THE

UNITED STATES COURT OF APPEALS

FOR THE THIRD CIRCUIT

———

No. 76-2165

CIVIL

———

EDWARD A. CUPP

APPELLANT

vs

COMMISSIONER OF INTERNAL REVENUE

APPELLEE

———

BRIEF OF APPELLANT

———

EDWARD A. CUPP
PRO SE
P. O. BOX 137
HOPWOOD, PA. 15445

TABLE OF CONTENTS

AUTHORITIES CITED

STATEMENT OF CASE

This is an appeal from a final order of the United States Tax Court rendered April 27, 1976.

Appellant-Petitioner would show unto this court that he did exercise and express his natural, fundamental, statutory and constitutional right of petitioning an agency of the United States for redress of grievances by preparing and submitting to the Appellee agency his Federal Income Tax forms 1040, the receipt of which has not been denied, on which the fifth amendment objection was taken to any question that might tend to incriminate him. The manner and form are described in the recent Supreme Court case of *Garner vs U.S.*, 47 L.Ed. 2nd 370 96 S. Ct. The manner and form of this filing became known and termed, by Appellee, as the "Fifth Amendment Protesters - Porth-Daly Type." (Pg. 168 B(c) - Ervin Report)

Appellant-Petitioner would further show that Appellee in 1969 established within its agency an organization known as "THE SPECIAL SERVICE STAFF." The history, fuction and dissolution of said organization is fully described in the publication POLITICAL INTELLIGENCE IN THE INTERNAL REVENUE SERVICE — A DOCUMENTARY ANALYSIS PREPARED BY THE STAFF of the SUBCOMMITTEE ON CONSTITUTIONAL RIGHTS of the COMMITTEE ON THE JUDICIARY, UNITED STATES SENATE, NINETY-THIRD CONGRESS, SECOND SESSION (U.S. Government Printing Office, Washington, D.C. 1974) herein referred to as the Ervin Report.

Appellant-Petitioner would show the report is incorporated into this brief as if fully set out therein, more specifically pp. 49-51, 164-178. Additional documentary proof concerning the SPECIAL SERVICE STAFF has recently been brought to light in the hearings before the SELECT COMMITTEE TO STUDY GOVERNMENTAL OPERATION WITH RESPECT TO INTELLIGENCE ACTIVITIES OF THE UNITED STATES SENATE, 94th CONGRESS, FIRST SESSION. hereinafter referred to as the "Church Report" and more specifically set out at pages 837 thru 920 of Book III of the Final Report, pages 89 thru 102 of Book II of said report, Volume 3 in its entirety and Volume 6 in its entirety; such material is fully incorporated in this brief as if fully set out therein.

The conspiracy between the administrative branch of government and the judicial branch of government referred to in Book III of the Final Report of the "Church Report", page 58 and entitled "INTERFERENCE WITH JUDICIAL PROCESS" has been recently verified by the release of documents published in the newspaper "SPOTLIGHT", dated September 13, 1976 and photocopies of said publication are included in the Appendix (pgs. 83-86).

The "SPECIAL SERVICE STAFF" was "allegedly" disbanded when its illegal and unconstitutional activities were uncovered and disclosed in the "Ervin Report," but there were some 380 persons or cases who were "selectively prosecuted" because they exercised their constitutional rights; the identity and disposition of those 380 persons or cases have not yet been identified. (See page 51 of said Ervin Report.)

Appellant-Petitioner would show that he believes that he is one of the 380 persons who has been allegedly "selectively prosecuted" because of his exercise of a constitutional right but all his efforts, including a request for a Subpoena Duces Tecum (See Appendix, P. 40). have been systematically denied.

Appellant-Petitioner would further show that he has made requests under the Freedom of Information Act for said information, and as of this date no information has been forthcoming. (See Appendix, P.-)

Appellant would show that the Appellee, through its Special Service Staff, was so intent in stifling the exercise of first amendment freedoms that it embarked on a series of illegal acts designed to punish Appellant and others. Instead of responding to the petition for redress of grievances as filed by Appellant-Petitioner, Appellant-Petitioner was greeted with an arbitrary assessment in the form of a Notice of Deficiency.

At the hearing on the deficiency notice, February 8, 1973, which should have been conducted under Title 5 of USC Section 500 et seq., Appellant-Petitioner's rights to due process were completely violated. To wit:

1. The hearing, as a tribunal or forum, did not have the

jurisdiction or legal capacity to adjudicate grievances as set forth by Petitioner on his 1969, 1970 and 1971 Federal Tax Returns as filed nor on his written or oral protests as presented.

2. The persons that conducted the hearing were not qualified nor did they have authority to adjudicate objections raised by Petitioner.

3. The persons conducting the hearing limited the scope of Petitioner's defenses to monetary matters and refused to consider other defenses put forth by Petitioner as provided by 5 U.S.C. Section 554 and 557. (See response to 30-day letter, paragraph 5(e) of Petition.) (Appendix, p.7)

4. The persons conducting the hearing acted as investigator, adversaries, judge and jury.

5. Petitioner was denied services and counsel of his choosing contrary to 5 U.S.C. Section 500 (d)(1), 5 U.S.C. Section 555 and 5 U.S.C. Section 557 and Amendments I and V of the United States Constitution.

6. By the denial by the agents of the Appellee to Appellant-Petitioner's request to inspection of the full and complete record as provided by 5 U.S.C. Section 556 and 5 U.S.C. Section 557.

7. That by letter dated February 10, 1973, addressed to agent James J. Kofmehl, he again requested an inspection of

STATEMENT OF ISSUE NUMBER I

DOES THE FORMATION AND ACTIVITIES OF AN ORGANIZA-TION WITHIN THE INTERNAL REVENUE SERVICE, KNOWN AS "THE SPECIAL SERVICE STAFF," WHOSE ONLY FUNC-TION WAS TO STIFLE DISSENT AND TO DISCOURAGE AND PUNISH PERSONS SUCH AS THE APPELLANT-PETITIONER FOR THE EXERCISE OF THEIR RIGHTS UNDER THE FIRST AMENDMENT CONSTITUTE A VIOLATION OF APPELLANT'S RIGHTS UNDER AMENDMENT I AND DOES IT CONSTITUTE A FRAUD ON THIS COURT BY COMING IN WITH "UNCLEAN HANDS?"

Appellant would show that on July 2, 1969 there was established within the Internal Revenue Service an internal unit which became known as the Special Service Staff. This secret

intelligence agency came to light in spring of 1973 when an
unmarked envelope was received in the mail by Senator Sam J.
Ervin. This envelope contained a copy of a memorandum from the
North Atlantic Regional Commission of the Internal Revenue
Service and addressed to all District Directors of the Internal
Revenue Service. The Senator was shocked at the objectives and
scope of this secret intelligence agency, and a full-scale inquiry
was launched by the Constitutional Rights Sub-Committee on the
Committee of the Judiciary of the United States Senate. The
investigation lasted one and one-half years and is detailed in an
analysis in the publication Political Intelligence In The Internal
Revenue Service: The Special Service Staff (December 1974).
Certain individuals and groups were "targeted" for the Special
Service Staff's attention, and a total of 8,585 individual files and
over 3000 organizational dossiers were collected.

STATEMENT OF ISSUE NUMBER II

WAS THE TAX COURT IN ERROR IN NOT DETERMINING
THAT THE FILING OF THE FEDERAL INCOME TAX FORM
1040, IN THE MANNER CALLED BY THE APPELLEES THE
PORTH-DALY TYPE, BY THE APPELLANT WITH THE IN-
INTERNAL REVENUE SERVICE CONSTITUTED A PETITION
FOR REDRESS OF GRIEVANCES UNDER AMENDMENT I OF
THE CONSTITUTION OF THE UNITED STATES AND THAT
THAT PETITION WAS RECEIVED BY APPELLEES?

Appellant-Petitioner would show, as delineated in paragraph
4 of the Petition (Appendix, p.2), that he filed his 1969 Federal
Tax return in a manner designed to test its constitutionality; that
he filed his 1970 Federal Tax return in a manner designed to test
its constitutionality; that he filed his 1971 Federal Tax return in a
manner designed to test its constitutionality, exercising his first
amendment rights for redress of grievances in the manner
prescribed in United States vs Sullivan, 274 U.S. 259, 71 L.Ed.
1037 (1927) and Garner vs U.S., 47 L.Ed. 2nd 370 (1976).

The manner of filing used by Appellant-Petitioner has been
labeled by Appellees as the "Porth-Daly" type (page 168-Ervin
Report).

Appellant-Petitioner has cited *New York Times Co. vs United States*, 403 U.S. 713, 29 L.Ed. 2nd 822 to show that first amendment rights occupy a preferred position in our constitutional scheme. He has further stated the right to speak and petition extends not only to appeals to the legislative and executive branches of the government but to the judicial as well and has cited *California Transport vs Trucking Unlimited*, 404 U.S.

STATEMENT OF ISSUE NUMBER III

WAS THE TAX COURT IN ERROR IN NOT DETERMINING THAT THE APPELLANT'S RIGHTS UNDER AMENDMENTS I, V AND VII WERE VIOLATED WHEN THE APPELLEE AGENCY, UPON RECEIPT OF PETITION, FAILED TO PROVIDE FOR A FULL AND COMPLETE HEARING AND INSTEAD DID PENALIZE APPELLANT FOR HIS EXERCISE OF HIS FIRST AMENDMENT RIGHTS BY MAKING AN ASSESSMENT WHICH EXCEEDED THE AMOUNT OF TWENTY DOLLARS ($20.00) WITHOUT A TRIAL BY JURY IN VIOLATION OF HIS SEVENTH AMEND-MENT RIGHTS, SUCH ASSESSMENT AMOUNTING TO A BILL OF PAINS AND PENALTIES?

Appellant would show that he was using the Federal Income Tax Form 1040 in exercising his right to petition for redress of grievances under Amendment I of the United States Constitution for the years involved. Appellant was using *United States vs Sullivan*, 274 U.S. 259, 71 L.Ed. 1037 as authority for presenting his protest to the administrative agency. The admonition of the Sullivan case is:

"But if the Defendant desires to test that or any other point he should have tested it in the return so that it could be passed on."

It is respectfully submitted that the legal significance of filing tax returns in this manner is to join issue with the agency, for resolution of issues presented.

It is respectfully submitted if one has a right to petition, then under our system of representative government, there is a corresponding duty to respond. It becomes the duty of agency petitioned to provide a full and complete hearing on the issues presented: 2 Am Jur 2nd "Administrative Law,"

STATEMENT OF ISSUE NUMBER IV

WAS THE TAX COURT IN ERROR IN NOT DETERMINING THAT THE FILING OF THE FEDERAL INCOME TAX FORM 1040 WITH THE INTERNAL REVENUE SERVICE, IN THE MANNER CALLED BY THE APPELLEE "THE PORTH-DALY" TYPE, CONSTITUTED A PROPER EXERCISE OF FIFTH AMENDMENT RIGHTS AGAINST SELF INCRIMINATION AS PROVIDED BY GARNER VS U.S., 47 L.ED. 2ND 370.

There is no question that Federal Income Tax form 1040 was received by Appellee agents for the years involved (1969, 1970 & 1971) on which Appellant-Petitioner exercised his right against self incrimination, relying upon Amendment V of the United States Constitution.

Petitioner would also show that the suggestion that the constitutional privilege to refuse to answer does not extend to any but criminal cases is absolutely without foundation in precedent or logic: Re Shera, 114 Fed. 207; Re Feldstein, 103 Fed. 269, 2 N.B.N. Rep. 982; Re Kanter, 117 Fed. 356; Re Scott, 95 Fed. 815; Carey v Donohue, 126 C.C.A. 254, 209 Fed. 328, 332; Re Rosser, 96 Fed. 305; Re Nachman, 114 Fed. 995; United States v Goldstein, 132 Fed. 789; Re Walsh, 104 Fed. 518, 2 B.N.N. Rep. 1031; United States v. Rhodes, 212 Fed. 518; Re Harris 221 U.S. 274, 55 L.Ed. 732, 31 Sup. ct. Rep. 557; Johnson v. United States, 228 U.S. 457, 57 L. Ed. 919, 47 L.R.A. (N.S.) 263, 33 Sup. Ct. Rep. 572; People ex rel. Taylor v. Forbes, 143 N.Y. 227, 38 N.E. 303; Re Rouse, 221 N.Y. 86, 116 N.E. 782; People ex rel. Lewisohn v. O'Brien, 176 N.Y. 253, 68 N.E.

STATEMENT OF ISSUE NUMBER V

DOES THE DENIAL OF APPELLANT OF SERVICES OF COUNSEL OF HIS CHOOSING, AT BOTH THE HEARING AND AGAIN IN TAX COURT TRIAL, OF A PERSON WHO IS NOT A LICENSED ATTORNEY, VIOLATE APPELLANT'S RIGHTS UNDER THE FIRST AMENDMENT AND THE DUE PROCESS CLAUSE OF AMENDMENT V?

Appellant would show unto this court that he did request counsel of his choosing at the calender date proceeding on January 27, 1975 and again at the opening of the Tax Court Trial on January 30, 1975 (T-p.2) and was refused that request by the trial judge.

Appellant would also show that there is an absence of qualification or requirement for counsel in the Constitution of the United States.

Appellant would also show that there are no actual requirements that Federal District Court judges or Supreme Court judges be licensed lawyers. Such a situation creates a double standard and is therefore unconstitutional on its face in that it violates appellant's rights under Amendment I and the "due process" clause of Amendment V of the United States Constitution.

In discussing right to counsel, the United States Supreme Court held: "His right to be heard through his own counsel is unqualified." (*Chandler vs Fretag*, 348 US: 3)

The appellee agency accepts "accountants" as counsel and such accountants need not be licensed lawyers.

STATEMENT OF ISSUE NUMBER VI

THE TAX COURT JUDGE WAS IN ERROR IN NOT RE-CUSING HERSELF AND IN NOT TRANSFERRING THE CASE TO A COURT OF COMPETENT JURISDICTION.

Appellant would show that he requested Judge Irene Scott to recuse herself on the occasion of the calender date hearing on January 27, 1975 and again at the opening of the trial on January 30, 1975. (T., p. 4 et seq.)

The basis of the challenge was that Judge Scott was a defendant in two cases involving appellant, (W. Dist. of Pa. No. 75-56 and 75-589) and therefore biased.

Appellant's position was supported by brief. (Appendix, pp. 87-94)

Appellant would also show that Tax Court judges are not confirmed according to the Constitution of the United States (Article 2, Sec. 2, para. 2) and therefore acting without constitutional authority.

In not recusing herself under 28 USC, Sec. 144, Judge Scott continued to the termination of the trial and subsequent hearings and actions in spite of lack of constitutional authority.

The Opinion (Appendix, p.46) clearly indicates that the Tax Court in the instant case acted in concert with the appellee agency and thus became an adversary to the appellant instead of a neutral arbiter. The effect was that the appellee agency judged the acts of their own agency and consistently demonstrated bias throughout the trial.

STATEMENT OF ISSUE NUMBER VII

THE TAX COURT JUDGE WAS IN PARTIAL ERROR IN DECIDING THAT THE GOLD AND SILVER STANDARD REQUIREMENT OF ARTICLE I, SEC, 10, PARA, 1 OF THE UNITED STATES CONSTITUTION APPLIED TO STATES BUT NOT TO THE FEDERAL GOVERNMENT.

Appellant would show that in stating in her Opinion (Appendix, p.60) that the gold and silver requirement applied to States but not to the Federal government. Judge Scott was only partially correct.

Since there is no gold or silver in general circulation (since March 18, 1968) such reasoning attempts to establish an impossibility.

In response to a letter to the Treasury Department of the United States, requesting a clarifying definition of a "dollar", appellant was informed by letter (Appendix, p.100) that Congress adopted the "dollar" as the monetary unit of the United States and fixed its value in 1786 at 375.64 grains of pure silver.

Assuming that the information received is the latest lawful definition, appellant can find no way to comply with the requirements of the States as stated in Judge Scott's Opinion.

There is no lawful basis for requiring one species of "money" for the States and another for the Federal government. The Federal government being the instrument of the several states.

CONCLUSION

As an American citizen, appellant has an inherent right under both the Federal and State Constitutions to disagree with his government. If he chooses to disagree, we have established procedures which are in accordance with law and are peaceful to bring that disagreement to the attention of government or its agencies.

The guarantee of that right to gain the attention of government is embodied in the Right to Petition for Redress of Grievances clause of Amendment I of the Constitution of the United States. If that right, not given by government, but secured and guaranteed by government, is stripped from him, appellant must presume that all other inalienable rights have been stripped also.

As the "Ervin" and "Church" reports are read, it brings to mind the quote from CICERO in 42 B.C., wherein he stated:

"A Nation can survive its fools, and even the ambitious. But it cannot survive treason from within. An enemy at the gates is less formidable, for he is known and he carries his banners openly. But the traitor moves among those within the gates freely, his sly whispers rustling through all the alleys, heard in the very halls of government itself. For the traitor appears not traitor; he speaks in the accents familiar to his victims, and he wears their face and their garments, and he appeals to the baseness that lies deep in the hearts of all men. He rots the soul of a nation; he works secretly and unknown in the night to undermine the pillars of a city; he infects the body politic so that it can no longer resist. A murderer is less to be feared."

The Tax Court was in error in ruling for the appellee agency in the instant case in light of the evidence presented at the time of trial as well as the constitutional issues raised by the appellant.

It is respectfully requested that the case be remanded to the Tax Court with instructions that appellees herein be required to give appellant a full and complete administrative hearing as per Title 5 USC, with an administrative determination on all issues raised by appellant on his tax returns and in his written and oral protests raised before the appellee agency. It is requested that a mandate be issued assessing all costs and disbursements against appellees.

C.   COMMENTARY ON DR. CUPP

From letters received from him and from news items concerning Dr. Cupp in the press, we learn that his appeal was still pending in 1978; that he was still continuing his medical practice as before; that he did not deposit any money in bank accounts; that he had divested himself of all seizable property or assets of any kind; and that, no matter what the courts or the IRS may decide to do, it will never be possible for them to lay hands on a single dollar pursuant to any judgment or assessment that may be levied against him.

In one letter, he wrote that no matter how many deficiency judgments the IRS obtains against him, there will be nothing for them to seize except "a bag of wind." And he added that even if they can obtain a criminal conviction against him, he thinks he can defeat that also.

Eleven   The Resistance of the Independents

A.   THE MIDDLE CLASS VS.
THE BUREAUCRACY

One of the most unfortunate results of the federal income tax is that it has done more to lower the general level of morality and political integrity than anything previously known in American history. It has been said that when an income tax was mentioned to Benjamin Franklin at the Constitutional Convention, he opposed it on the ground that it would make liars and evaders of the people and a despotism of the government.

We have already defined the Middle Class as consisting technically of those who, to a greater or lesser degree, are in business for themselves; whose labor and money are invested partly or entirely in their means of livelihood; whose economic rewards, which may become substantial, will be commensurate with their energy and wisdom; who ask nothing from government except the ordinary protection of life and property; who bitterly resent the interference and excessive burdens inflicted upon them by the bureaucracy; and who, since they are not subject to withholding, calculate their own income taxes when they make their 1040 returns. In this group, we find about thirteen million proprietors in 1978-79; there are also great numbers classified as professionals of various categories; and there are other millions, including farmers, landlords, consultants, salesmen, etc., who belong in the same general classification. We estimate the total number of Middle-Class adults, including spouses, at well over forty-five millions, who, should they unite in a political party, might well control the destiny of the nation.

The Internal Revenue Service, as we have pointed out, evinces a deep hostility toward these independents, not only because they resent Big-Brother Government, but even more because they cannot be adequately policed or controlled. And, since it cannot determine their incomes accurately, it has secreted a multitude of traps and snares in the Code for the purpose of destroying them even when, to the best of their knowledge and belief, they have paid their taxes in full.

We emphasize that it is almost impossible to overestimate the real and potential importance of this segment in our population; they are now and always have been the bedrock upon which any republican or responsible form of government must rest. However, since every bureaucracy seeks to establish an authoritarian, central state, it is by its very nature the sworn enemy of the independent entrepreneur. The bureaucrat desires, first, large corporations, which can be controlled, taken into partnership, or nationalized — more or less intact — and so made an integral portion of the super-state; and, second, wage-workers, who, since they are never required to make economic decisions, seldom do any thinking for themselves in the political sphere and can, therefore, more easily be manipulated. In this respect, let us note, it is not the size of an income but its nature and source which are determinative in developing the ideology of its recipient. A popcorn vendor, earning only a few dollars a day, may think clearly in politics and be deeply interested therein, while a skilled member of a trade union earning more per hour than the other does in a day, may be totally unconcerned over the nature of despotism, expanding government, and growing authoritarian control, since it is not necessary for him to make personal, economic, day-to-day decisions in prosecuting his means of livelihood and since it is not likely that some government bureaucrat will attempt to interfere with every aspect of his daily existence.

Any knowledgeable observer of the American scene since 1913, must comprehend how agencies created by the federal government — especially the Federal Reserve System, the Internal Revenue Service, the Office of Price Administration

under F. D. Roosevelt, the Occupational and Safety Health
Administration (OSHA) of the Seventies — were all established
to harass, impoverish, and, if possible, to destroy the Middle
Class. The OPA caused some seven million small landlords to lose
their properties, for which they had sacrificed so bitterly. The
Federal Reserve System has been employed to create successive
inflation and deflation, in wave after wave, in order to confiscate
Middle-Class assets, and thus prevent them from becoming the
basis for an independent and powerful political force. During and
following WW I, the Fed caused enormous inflation, easy money,
and seeming prosperity, which encouraged investors to improve
their properties by incurring debt. During the artificially
contrived deflation which followed, these debts could not be paid
and a general confiscation ensued in which hundreds of thousands
of entrepreneurs, especially farmers, were totally ruined.

During the Twenties, the Fed permitted prosperity to
continue for nearly eight years, during which millions again
created small estates; then, in 1926, it caused the stock market
speculation which ended in the debacle of 1929, which, in turn,
was followed by the worst depression ever known, and which was
continued by manipulation for the purpose of liquidating real
estate, savings accounts, investments, the stock market,
insurance policies, the farmers — everyone and everything
except the governing financiers, who appropriated the fruits of
billions of hours of labor at about ten cents on the dollar.

The liquidation was accomplished by withdrawing almost all
money from circulation, making credit unobtainable, destroying
the value of real estate, causing universal bankruptcy, and
establishing an unemployment rate approaching eighty per cent.
Believe it or not, the Board of Governors of the Fed has the power
to re-create the same conditions any day it chooses. Now,
however, since people are beginning to understand the monetary
question at least to some degree there would probably, in case of
a severe depression, be a quick political revulsion, leading to
drastic reforms, including the repeal of the Federal Reserve Act
and basic reforms in the Internal Revenue Code and administration.

The agencies established by the federal government are

constantly attacking the economic base of the Middle Class in order to render it politically impotent. This can be done through inflation as well as by deflation: in the Thirties, the Fed accomplished this objective by banishing money, making most securities and nearly all real estate virtually worthless in the marketplace; in the Seventies, the same forces are achieving a similar result by flooding the market with currency that is gradually losing its buying power, a process which involves a vast repudiation of the national debt, a sharp decline in the value of savings accounts, insurance policies, annuities, accounts receivable, debts to be repaid, etc. At the same time, it increases the prices of homes, goods, services, etc., to a point where people cannot afford them at all, or can buy them only at a sacrifice which precludes the possibility of saving anything for the future.

During such periods of inflation, prices rise much faster than buying power; and living standards fall even with increased monetary income, as the Internal Revenue Service levies taxes at higher rates upon an ever-increasing portion of personal income. We see, therefore, that the federal government has a vested interest in continuous inflation. Also, in the meantime, as Social Security checks buy less and less, a shrinking number of contributors must pay more and more into a bankrupt system in order to sustain life for an ever-increasing number of recipients, who have actually become paupers under a program that reeks of approaching collapse.

By abolishing a solid, redeemable currency, the financiers who control the Fed manipulate not only the economy, but have placed a noose around the neck of every man, woman, and child in the nation. By increasing the available credit by seventy per cent on November 9, 1972 and by reducing interest rates at the same time, it created the subsequent inflation; and then, by restricting credit and doubling interest rates, in April, 1974, it brought on a depression and a catastrophic decline in the stock market which brought bankruptcy to thousands of small businessmen and eventually made billions of profit for those who manipulated these fluctuations in the financial world.

By and large, a numerous and prosperous Middle Class is our only protection against despotism, the only guarantee of continuing constitutional government. If this class can protect itself from bureaucratic destruction; preserve its financial base; enable itself to expand; organize into a unified political force, we may be able to create in the western world a solid and permanent bastion against communism, its sister-disease of socialism, and all other forms of authoritarian despotism.

In the formation of a great political party dedicated to freedom and constitutional government, the Middle Class will of course take the lead and be the solid base; however, it has millions of potential allies. Skilled workers will enroll in the movement because their interests are closely interwoven, as are, in fact, those of all who do useful work of any kind. Only parasites, extortionists, bureaucrats, political favorites, and other leeches on the body-politic will be opposed to a philosophy which advances the general welfare.

Should all the members of the great American Middle Class — none of whom are subject to withholding since they are self-employed — simultaneously and in desperation refuse to file any income-tax returns, the government would be absolutely helpless, and the entire present system of federal taxation would have to be abolished.

The principal objectives of the Middle-Class resistance therefore may be summarized as follows: (1) the termination of such taxation, at least on all earned income; (2) the replacement of the present Social Security System with a Universal Trust Plan; (3) the repeal of the Federal Reserve Act and its replacement with a constitutional monetary system; (4) the establishment of a solid currency that will maintain its value as a medium of exchange with little variation from year to year and generation to generation; (5) a central government limited to those activities specifically summarized and listed in the Constitution; (6) a sharp reduction in federal expenditures, a balanced budget, and the liquidation of the national debt; (7) a drastic reduction in the number of federal bureaucrats, who use nearly half of the revenues accruing from the personal federal income tax simply to maintain themselves; and (8) a Jeffersonian system, in which the federal government will concern itself only with foreign relations and the interrelationships between the states, leaving all other

activities to the states respectively, or to the people themselves.
The purpose of this work, therefore, is primarily to enable
members of the Middle Class not only to survive, but to become
more independent financially. The advice herein offered has
proved effective for this writer and many others. If absorbed and
followed, it can make the difference between success and
economic destruction.

B. A HOST OF INDEPENDENT ENTREPRENEURS

It is highly significant as well as encouraging that, in spite of
all efforts on the part of the federal government to limit or
prevent the growth of the middle class, it has continued to
increase rapidly since the Second World War. The accompanying
table demonstrates its expansion and economic importance.

PROPRIETORSHIPS IN THE UNITED STATES[A]

	1945	1965	1974
NUMBER	5,689,000	9,078,000	10,874,000
Receipts	$79,000,000,000	$199,385,000,000	$328,300,000,000
Net Profits	12,069,000,000	27,887,000,000	45,855,000,000
Av. Receipts	13,870	21,910	30,280
Av. Net Profit	2,110	3,084	4,217
Under $50,000 Businesses			10,321,000
Ratio			95.5%
Retail Establishments	1,414,546[B]	1,554,000	1,802,000
Receipts	NA	$77,860,000,000	$106,500,000,000
Profits	NA	5,019,000,000	5,900,000,000
Av. Receipts	NA	50,690	59,180
Av. Profits	NA	3,230	3,833
Service Establishments	559,559[C]	2,208,000	2,943,000
Receipts	$8,578,162,000	$29,789,000,000	$51,341,000,000
Av. Receipts	15,330	13,500	17,474
Profits	NA	11,008,000,000	17,200,000,000
Av. Profits	NA	5,000	5,850

A. Cf. SA 1963; ib. 1968 p. 473; and ib. 1977 pp. 550-551
B. 1956 SA p. 210, for year 1950.
C. Ib. p. 870 for 1948

The data in this table, which include every kind of individual non-agricultural enterprise, shows that sole proprietorships increased from 5,689,000 in 1945 to 10,874,000 in 1974; their receipts from $79 to $328 billion; and their net profits from $12 to nearly $46 billion, with average receipts rising from $13,870 to $30,280 and net profits from $2,110 to $4,247. Since these nets are extremely low, we are inclined to believe that substantial under-reporting must have been a common practice.

We find, further, that the number of such retail establishments grew from 1,414,546 to 1,802,000 between 1950 and 1974; and that during the nine years following 1965, their cash flow increased from $77.9 to $106.5 billion; their profits from $5 to $5.9 billion; their average income from $50,690 to $59,180, while their average net profits increased from $3,230 to $3,833. In the personal service division, the number of establishments increased from 559,559 in 1948 to 2,943,000 in 1974; receipts from $8.6 to $51.3 billion; meanwhile, the reported average cash flow increased only from $15,330 to $17,474, and the taxable income only from $5,000 in 1965 to $5,850 in 1974.

In addition to the 10,874,000 sole proprietorships existing in 1974 (which represented at least eleven million self-employed individuals and which have increased since then beyond the thirteen million mark), there are great numbers of others who definitely qualify as members of the middle class: for they operate independently, keep their own books, make their own economic decisions, are not subject to income or Social Security tax withholding, pay taxes only on the incomes they report, and are responsible for their own success or failure. Among these we may include the following (1975 *SA* pp. 360-63) as shown by the 1970 United States census:

OTHER SELF-EMPLOYED INDIVIDUALS

Farmers	1,810,000
Accountants	
Male	526,000
Female	187,000
Architects	55,000
Lawyers	260,000

Physicians	256,000
Dentists	88,000
Ministers, Religious Workers	228,000
Writers and Artists	550,000
Insurance Agents	403,000
Real Estate Brokers and Salesmen	181,000
Sales Representatives	990,000
TOTAL	5,534,000

Note also the following statistics covering rental investments of more than six million mostly small landlords, all of
whom operate such properties, obtain a portion or all of their
income from them, and thus definitely qualify for membership in
the middle class.

RENTAL HOUSING STATISTICS

Units in 1975 (1977 *SA* p. 789)	25,656,000
Average Annual Rent (*ib.*)	$1,644
Total Rentals	$42,178,464,000
Owners in 1969 (*Statistics of Income*, 14)	6,343,040
Rental Units Owned	20,227,000
Average Units per Owner	3.2
Reported Profits	$5,066,000,000
Reported Book Losses	2,263,000,000
Net Reported Profits	3,403,000,000
Average Taxable Income per Unit	168
Average Taxable Income per Landlord	537

These statistics are highly revealing: if we combine the total
for sole proprietorships, other self-employed categories, and the
owners of rental properties, we have a total of about 23 million;
together with spouses and adult children, they would comprise
nearly fifty million. And if we add to these, the managers,
administrators, and teachers who — though they receive salaries
— are nevertheless allied in interest and outlook with the middle
class as a while, we have a voting reserve far exceeding one-half
of all votes ever cast in an American election.

Anyone who believes that these millions of independents are reporting their incomes fully, is living in a dream-world; although the IRS is well aware that such underreporting exists, its exact extent is unknown and there is very little the Agency can do about it. There can be no doubt that such evasion is increasing rapidly, triggered, as it is, by inflation, onerous taxes, a general disenchantment with government in general, but particularly the federal, and a well-based suspicion that waste and corruption are rampant throughout the governmental structures of the nation.

C. THE MODUS OPERANDI

It is not too difficult for an independent businessman or woman to reduce his tax-burden. Anyone operating a retail establishment can simply enter 90 or 85 per cent of receipts in his books. If, at the end of the year, he thus shows a gross of $90,000 or of $85,000 instead of $100,000, his books will balance. On the basis of invoiced expenditures for merchandise, he therefore has a markup of perhaps fifty or sixty per cent instead of seventy-five or eighty. But this provides no practical way in which the IRS can establish fraud. Perhaps the merchant has sold some of his stock in sales at marked-down prices; perhaps he operates at a lower margin than his competitors because he has less overhead. At all events, without definite proof of fraud, the IRS cannot bring any charges or levy a deficiency assessment. Ironically, the clever chiseler goes free, while his honest counterpart is ruined by some trap.

In spite of the Marxian predictions that the middle class would be eliminated by the automatic developments within the capitalist system and despite every effort on the part of the Internal Revenue Service and other federal agencies to make such predictions come true, they simply refuse to fade away — in fact, they continue to increase in numbers as well as in financial importance. In 1948, there were 665,000 service establishments with receipts of $13.3 billion; in 1972, the number had increased to 1,590,000, of which only 68,000 had any payroll, but the total reported income of which was no less than $113 billion. (1977 *SA* 829.)

If the Internal Revenue Service could keep an operative

stationed in every retail or service establishment every minute of every day as well as in the office of every doctor, lawyer, and other professional, it might, with a force of two or three million spies, make an accurate accounting of their true incomes. But, since every auditor must show a return of at least $100 for every hour expended in audits, it is obvious that actual supervision of independent business is an impossibility.

How can IRS determine whether a hardware or paint merchant takes in $200 rather than $175 on an average day? Since it cannot, it must accept the return it receives, or, by its own efforts, determine that it is fraudulent. If it does this, it must bring charges that can be sustained by the rules of evidence before a jury, a proceeding which may cost the government thousands of hours of research and probably $100,000 of the taxpayers' money.

In the case of service establishments, such as barber, beauty, or auto repair shops, opportunities for underreporting are even more inviting. Since business invoices to them constitute no index by which to gauge the amount of their business, and since almost the entire income is for work performed, the IRS has no yardstick by which to measure revenue. How can it know whether a barber trims ten or thirty heads in a day or whether a mechanic gets $10 or $25 for doing a certain repair job? It has little or no information except what is furnished by the operator.

How can the IRS know whether a dentist or doctor takes in $50,000 or $75,000 a year? It cannot seize their medical records; it can only scan his return and attempt to obtain additional information from other sources, such as bank records — which, if precautions are taken — remain immune to such scrutiny, except by court order issued for probable cause and after a long period of appeals. How can the IRS or any other authority know if motels and tourist courts — of which there were 41,954 in 1967 — 38,508 active preprietors and only 637 with a regular payroll — average 20 or 25 daily clients? Obviously, no one except the proprietors can know the number of customers or the total income.

It is well known that a substantial portion of the entire American economy has gone "underground"; that is, it consists of unreported and therefore untaxed contract income performed by

individuals outside the wage-controlled cycle, which is subject to
Social Security and income-tax withholding. It is estimated that
tax-evasion in this area may now total tens of billions of dollars
and, if it continues to escalate, can destroy the entire current tax
and financial structure of the nation. One prestigious estimate
placed the amount at $200 billion.

D. THE RENTAL BUSINESS

In 1975, there were 77,563,000 housing units, of which
25,656,000 were rented, as noted on a previous page. In 1969,
there were 6,343,040 income tax returns covering 20,227,000
units, or 3.2 per owner. The net income from rents was
$5,066,000,000 and the net loss was $2,263,000,000, leaving a
taxable income of $3,403,000,000, or an average of $537 per owner
and $168 per unit. Of the 3,923,566 which reported net incomes,
2,336,225 had less than $10,000 net and 777,782 had no taxable
income at all; there were also 2,419,484 returns which showed net
paper losses averaging $911.

It is therefore obvious that we are here dealing with about
six million comparatively small owners of rental property; there
might possibly have been twice that number today had not the
OPA been used to destroy approximately seven million small
investors between 1942 and 1953. Even so, we find that owners
reported $42,178,464,000 in gross rental incomes in 1975 (1977 *SA*
780). The total is probably double this amount in 1980.

Since residential rents are not deductible from taxable
income there is no ready way in which such income may be
verified. Perhaps 60 to 70 per cent of such gross is deductible for
interest, taxes, utilities, repairs, depreciation, management, etc.;
and if one-half of the remaining revenue is unreported, the loss to
the Treasury could total nearly $10 billion.

E. THE LAW OF SURVIVAL

Hundreds of thousands of independents have been destroyed
by the government; but every day others appear, who are wiser
and wilier. They are keeping more and more of their own money
and surviving in spite of all the attempts by the IRS to increase
their taxes or seize their property.

For many years, I have observed the artifices to evade taxation which have become more prevalent ever since income-tax exactions became so onerous under Franklin D. Roosevelt. The powerful, the wealthy and the favored have their loopholes, as they had from the beginning; but now, small proprietors and entrepreneurs have developed their own effective immunities.

Some of the income-tax work I did in Detroit was for taxpayers with depreciable property and commercial incomes. I remember in particular one woman who operated a rooming house and who came to me year after year with a very neat set of books, showing income, deductions, and expenditures. I never suspected fraud on the part of this prim, conventional lady; but when her returns were completed, her taxable income generally was less than $300. Then, one day, a man appeared who explained that his wife had recently died, and would I now make out a final return? One look at the books he had with him showed that her actual taxable income totalled several thousand dollars! Shortly thereafter, I learned of a woman who operated a successful beauty shop and who reported *an annual net loss*, to offset income from other sources which might be traced or documented; and I heard of a doctor who had stashed away several hundred thousand dollars of unreported income under assumed names in safety boxes in other cities. And suddenly it dawned upon me that there must be thousands all around me engaged in the same method of asset-conservation: not because of any ideological persuasion or because they were crooks in the usual sense (since they were perfectly honest in dealing with their fellow men) but simply because they wished to retain their own hard-earned money. And if there were many practising such slippery arts in 1948-49, their numbers and expertise must have increased greatly before 1979-80.

The principal reason the IRS insists on examining bank accounts is, of course, to discover whether deposits exceed reported income. However, canny individuals have learned that there are simple methods by which to guard against this peril. If, in the case of the hardware merchant mentioned above, his gross income was $100,000 instead of the $90,000 or $85,000 he reported, he would, of course, not deposit the $10,000 or $15,000 of excess in his checking or other banking account, which might some day be examined by the IRS. Instead, he would lay it aside or disburse it in cash; he and his family could spend it for a variety of personal benefits, such as better food, clothing, entertainment, travel, and comforts which they could not otherwise afford. By this method, there is no tell-tale trail leading to deposits or investments; and it is virtually impossible for the IRS to prove that the income ever existed.

If the amount of such self-exempted income continues to grow, it can be placed in depositories outside the taxpayer's bank, perhaps under assumed names or in those of close relatives or friends; and, in due course, the owner can purchase tax-exempt bonds under the same or another alias and receive income from the coupons in the same manner. Since such securities are exempt from both taxation and disclosure, and since revenues from them are not reported on 1099s, there is little chance that the government can discover their existence.

If such sums should grow into substantial totals, there are still ways to conceal them and even to enjoy the income from them with comparative security. It is being done constantly on a wide scale. Although aware of this, the IRS is powerless to prevent it. For in such situations, which involve criminal fraud, the burden of proof shifts from the taxpayer to the Agency; and the evader, in most instances, need merely say nothing to remain immune to punishment.

F. SUMMARY

That independent enterprise constitutes a very significant segment of the American economy cannot be questioned. And we believe that a tax-revolt by millions of these — contractors, proprietors, farmers, and professionals — would perhaps do more than anything else to bring the IRS to its knees. It is simply impossible for it to police them; it cannot by any conceivable method determine or document their exact gross or net income; and if they engage in a general practice of understating income, there is simply no means by which they can be brought to punishment.

There is no doubt that literally millions have additional incomes from odd jobs or subsidiary services of some kind. Women may do housework without reporting it; boys can mow lawns, clean yards, run errands, and perform many kindred tasks, never reported; girls can work as babysitters; mechanics can repair cars for neighbors; plumbers, carpenters, paperhangers, painters, and electricians can moonlight; and people can rent out a room or two or even a housekeeping unit or an apartment without reporting it. We have no doubt that billions of dollars stem from such unreported and therefore untaxed activity.

We predict that the most powerful forces which will compel a drastic reform in our income-tax laws will consist (1) of the tens of millions of wage-earners who will report a sufficient number of allowances to avoid all federal income taxation and who, since no refund is to be expected, will then "forget" to file a return; (2) of the millions of independents whose incomes cannot be documented and who refuse to file at all or understate their incomes; and (3) of increasing numbers of individuals who will avoid taxation by utilizing the legal loopholes in the Code.

Finally, we believe that, as the general public awakens to the fact that the administration of the whole system is not only unconstitutional but also unjust, they will no longer submit; and it will have to be radically transformed or abolished altogether.

We have no doubt, furthermore, that, as a result of fraud, underreporting, or failure to file or divulge income at all, there is now a loss to the Treasury of at least $150 billion a year — which is in addition to the $70 or $80 billion which escapes because of the loopholes in the Code.

An enormous increase in non-taxable barter and exchange of labor and goods has occurred: farmers trade produce for items available in stores; plumbers and carpenters exchange services. The list is endless and the possibilities highly inviting.

As the "leakage" continues to grow, the Code will become more and more unenforceable; those who cannot escape will become more and more restive, frustrated, and wrathful. We believe that eventually there will be an explosion which will force the Congress to make drastic revisions in the Code, or which will accomplish its summary abolition.

Twelve   An Alternative to the Income Tax

A. BROKEN PROMISES

In order to achieve ratification for the Sixteenth Amendment, its proponents declared with solemnity in 1909-13 that it would be simple, just, and equitable and that no tax would ever be imposed on any portion of income necessary to sustain a decent, contemporary standard of living; in fact, it was understood that only large, unearned incomes would ever be subject to such taxation, except during a national emergency, such as war. In 1916, exemptions of $3,000 for single persons and $4,000 for families were established — tantamount to $15,000 and $20,000 in 1978-79. The tax levy was one per cent on the first $20,000 of taxable income; two per cent at the $50,000 level; and the highest rate of six per cent began at $500,000. I happen to have in my possession a copy of the very simple one-page form which was used. Had the system continued on this basis, its enforcement would have been comparatively easy nor would this book ever have been written.

However, beginning with the Roosevelt era, income-tax laws became more and more oppressive, complex, and discriminatory. No man living can now even pretend to understand the Internal Revenue Code as a whole; it contains thousands of sections, subsections, paragraphs, and sub-paragraphs, in addition to clauses, many of which are so complex, confusing, and obscurantist in language that neither courts nor experts can agree concerning their meaning. I have been trying for years to obtain a statement from the Agency as to whether or not a certain definite transaction would or would not involve a tax-liability;

and, although I have received single-spaced letters filling many pages, there has been no answer to my question. Then, to supplement the Code itself, there are some 40,000 pages of Regulations, most of which are not only unpublished, but inaccessible to the public; yet they are used by agents as if they were part of the congressional statute. In addition, the courts have handed down thousands of opinions attempting to explain or clarify the provisions of the Code. Nevertheless, the most illiterate person is expected to know it fully, since ignorance of the law protects no one. Although private tax-preparers must sign and inscribe their Social Security number on any return they prepare, no IRS agent will do so. Furthermore, the latter can never be held accountable for misstatements to a taxpayer or for any error in computing tax-liability. It seems that the only persons immune to punishment for ignorance of the law are those hired to enforce it.

For its operation, the Service receives an annual appropriation of about $3 billion; by conservative estimate, it costs the taxpayers at least an equal sum simply to prepare their returns and fight the IRS, a situation which has spawned an army of tax-preparers, consultants, experts, specialized lawyers, and other parasites whose function it is to assist or betray taxpayers in their battles for survival.

B. ANOTHER METHOD OF TAXATION

One of the most frequent questions asked when we appear on radio or T-V programs is how the federal government could operate should the income tax be abolished. We have no hesitation in replying that other sources of revenue presently available for this purpose could be utilized and would be sufficient merely by discontinuing some of the wasteful and unconstitutional activities of the federal government. A sum at least equal to the entire amount generated by the personal income tax is consumed in the support of the federal bureaucracy, for interest on the national debt, and in the payment of unconstitutional subsidies to individuals, private corporations, and other levels of government. Of $500 billion in 1979-80 revenue, less than half derives from personal and corporate income taxation. If the government were to operate on a constitutional basis, its income from sources other than this would be ample.

However, even if we should concede, for the sake of argument, that the federal government must continue to operate with a budget of $532 billion or more, we can easily point to an obvious alternative: a general transactions tax to be levied on personal services, the sale of consumer goods, and the exchange of capital assets, including securities, would be infinitely more fair, economical non-discriminatory, productive, and far less onerous than the existing federal system of taxation. The rich, who now pay very little, would contribute their fair share on large purchases, on capital exchanges, and in security dealings; but there would be no tax on employer profits or dividends — either to corporations or to recipients — and the poor, who buy little, would pay only a little. And, since the cost of all goods and services would be reduced by thirty per cent in the market place, this alternative tax would create an enormous saving for all low and middle-income-class families and individuals.

In 1973, state and city sales and use taxes, which averaged four per cent and were levied in forty-four states, produced $46,098,000,000. A nationwide five-per-cent tax would thus have produced about $70 billion; and had this been extended to the sales of real property, securities, and professional and other services, this sum would have surpassed $100 billion. By 1979-80, this would total at least $120 billion. As we have shown, the termination of its own taxes would reduce federal expenditures by $100 billion. It is therefore obvious that a general transactions tax of five per cent would be sufficient to maintain even the wasteful and unconstitutional activities now being carried on by the Washington colossus. If these were terminated there would be no need for either the personal or the corporate federal income tax nor yet for any other kind of tax to replace them.

If a general transactions tax were to replace the present federal income tax, every person would pay his fair share and the Treasury would obtain the same income at perhaps one-third of the present cost to the people, as we have already demonstrated. However, great as the economic benefits would be, these would

be overshadowed by other advantages; at a single stroke, the
uncertainty, the terror, the discrimination, the invasion of
privacy, the universal imperative to cheat and lie, would be
terminated.

Let us for a moment contrast the administration and
collection of a state sales and use tax with the operation of the
federal income tax. The former is so simple that a statutory
enactment could be printed on one or two pages; it can be
collected at extremely low cost to the government; and who ever
heard of a tax-expert receiving a huge fee for adjudicating a
sales-tax dispute? The sales-tax law, like the Constitution, is so
clear that not even a child can misunderstand it. In general, it is
fair and equitable to everyone. It is marvellously productive and
economical.

On the other hand, the federal income-tax laws, regulations,
and court decisions constitute a vast jungle totally beyond
comprehension; the most charitable statement we can make
concerning this statute is that it is uneconomic, incomprehensible, destructive, discriminatory, time-consuming, nerve-
wracking, and unconstitutional.

Our Founding Fathers considered excise taxes —
comparable to a sales tax — when equally imposed, constitutional; had anyone then proposed such an income tax as we now
have, he would have been hooted into silence; and had Congress
passed and attempted to enforce a statute similar to our present
Internal Revenue Code, the people would instantly have reacted
in armed revolt. The Whiskey Rebellion of 1793 would have been
almost as nothing in comparison.

The proponents of federal income taxation declare that sales
taxes fall most heavily on the poor and that only levies on large
incomes can force the rich to pay their fair share. No greater lie,
however, was ever concocted: the fact is that the rich become the
super-rich because of the loopholes planted in the Code for this
very purpose and that they and a multitude of other favorites
avoid at least $70 billion in federal taxation. Since taxes on
production are paid by consumers in the form of increased costs
for goods and services, they fall most heavily on those whose
incomes must be expended largely for food, clothing, housing,

and other necessities. It falls very lightly on those who have large, unearned revenues and vast accumulations of wealth.

C. THE CASE AGAINST THE FEDERAL INCOME TAX

The case against the present federal tax-structure is so complete and definitive that people in general have begun to comprehend its indefensibility. A Harris Poll taken in 1972 revealed that even then seventy-four per cent of the people would have sympathized with a national tax-strike. Although this book is not concerned *per se* with the tax-rebellion, we should at least note that it already involves millions of people and reaches into all political persuasions. We would say that its causes stem from the following convictions or persuasions:

(1) That the IR Code is filled with discriminatory inequities.

(2) That the crushing burden of federal taxation falls most heavily upon the middle classes.

(3) That the federal government wastes or misuses at least $100 billion annually.

(4) That the Code violates various provisions in the Bill of Rights.

(5) That the IRS seizes property without due process of law in direct violation of the Fifth Amendment.

(6) That the esoteric nature of the Code places it beyond ordinary comprehension and enables IRS agents to deceive taxpayers by misinterpretation.

(7) That it costs the taxpayers exorbitant sums to defend themselves against illegal assessments and that they cannot recover their costs in so doing.

(8) That IRS agents may not be held responsible or accountable for illegal or unethical acts committed against taxpayers.

(9) That the Code is filled with irrational, illogical, and contradictory traps and snares used to destroy independent business.

(10) That money collected by the IRS is used for political subversion.

(11) That the IRS is the conduit for channelling money into the Federal Reserve System, which, in turn, is controlled by

international financiers.

(12) That the IRS is used to finance ridiculous federal expenses, such as the $532-billion budget for 1979-80.

(13) That money is used to finance absurd research projects, such as the $95,000 given to two professors to investigate brothels in a South American country.

(14) That the federal income tax has, in effect, transformed the central government into a vast system of extortion and bribery, operated primarily for the benefit of bureaucrats and other parasites.

This rebellion is in no sense a movement to overthrow the law; on the contrary, its purpose is to enforce the Constitution against those who are undermining and destroying it. Its aim is to re-establish ideals and principles which are not yet utterly extinguished, even if the Constitution is now shamefully ignored.

APPENDIX

Material Which May Be Used By Taxpayers

STATEMENTS BY THOMAS JEFFERSON

Letter to Major John Cartwright, June 5, 1824:

"With respect to our State and Federal governments, I do not think their relations correctly understood by foreigners. They generally suppose the former subordinate to the latter. But this is not the case. They are co-ordinate departments of one simple and integral whole. To the State governments are reserved all legislation and administration, in affairs which concern their own citizens only, and to the federal government is given whatever concerns foreigners, or the citizens of the other States: these functions alone being made federal. The one is the domestic, the other the foreign branch of our government; neither having control of the other ..."

Letter to John Taylor, November 26, 1798:

"I wish it were possible to obtain a single amendment to our Constitution . . . . I mean an additional article, taking from the federal government their power of borrowing."

Letter to Albert Gallatin, October 11, 1809:

"I consider the fortunes of our republic as depending in an eminent degree, on the extinguishment of the whole debt before we engage in any war; because, that done, we shall have reserves enough to improve our country in peace and defend it in war, without recurring either to new taxes or loans. But if the debt should once be swollen to formidable size, the entire discharge shall be despaired of, and we shall be committed to the English career of debt, corruption, and rottenness ...."

From the First Eppes Letter, June 24, 1813:

"The earth belongs to the living, not the dead. The will and the power of men expire with their lives, by nature's law ... Each generation has the usufruct of the earth during the period of its continuance ... We may consider each generation as a distinct nation, with a right, by the will of the majority, to bind themselves, but none to bind the succeeding generation ...."

THE PROTECTION OF TAXPAYER RECORDS IN
THE HANDS OF THIRD PARTIES,
added to the Tax Reform Act of 1976

SECTION 7609

SPECIAL PROCEDURES FOR THIRD-PARTY SUMMONSES
(a) NOTICE. –
   (1) IN GENERAL. – If –
     (A) Any summons described in subsection (c) is served
on any person who is a third-party recordkeeper,
and
     (B) the summons requires the production of any
portion of records made or kept of the business
transactions or affairs of any person (other than the
the person summoned) who is identified in the description of the records contained in the summons, then
notice of the summons shall be given to any person
so identified within 3 days of the day on which such
service is made, but no later than the 14th day before
the day fixed in the summons as the day upon which
such records are to be examined. Such notice shall be
accompanied by a copy of the summons which has
been served and shall contain directions for staying
compliance with the summons under subsection (b)(2).

   (2) SUFFICIENCY OF NOTICE. – Such notice shall be
sufficient if, on or before such third day, such notice
is served in the manner provided in section 7603
(relating to service of summons) upon the person
entitled to notice, or is mailed by certified or registered mail to the last known address of such person,
or, in the absence of a last known address, is left with
the person summoned ...

   (3) THIRD-PARTY RECORDKEEPER DEFINED. – For
this subsection, the term 'third-party recordkeeper'
means

(A) any mutual savings bank, cooperative bank, domestic building and loan association, or other savings institution . . . any bank . . . or any credit union . . .
(B) any consumer reporting agency . . .;
(C) any person extending credit through the use of credit cards or similar devices;
(D) any broker . . . ;
(E) any attorney; and
(F) any accountant.

(4) EXCEPTIONS. — Paragraph (1) shall not apply to any summons —
(A) served on a person with respect to whose liability the summons is issued, or any officer or employee of such person,
(B) to determine whether or not records of the business transactions or affairs of an identified person have been made or kept, or
(C) described in subsection (f).

(5) NATURE OF SUMMONS. — Any summons to which this subsection applies (and any summons in aid of collection described in subsection (c) (2) (B)) shall identify the taxpayer to whom the summons relates or the other person to whom the records pertain and shall provide such other information as will enable the person summoned to locate the records required under the summons.

(b) RIGHT TO INTERVENE: RIGHT TO STAY COMPLIANCE. —

(1) INTERVENTION. — Notwithstanding any other law or rule of law, any person who is entitled to notice of a summons under subsection (a) shall have the right to intervene in any proceeding with respect to the enforcement of such summons under section 7604.

(2) RIGHT TO STAY COMPLIANCE. — Notwithstanding any other law or rule of law, any person who is entitled to notice or a summons under subsection (a) shall have the right to stay compliance with the summons if, not later than the 14th day after the day such notice is given in the manner provided in subsection (a) (2) —
(A) notice in writing is given to the person summoned not to comply with the summons, and
(B) a copy of such notice not to comply with the summons is mailed by registered or certified mail to such person and to such office as the Secretary may direct in the notice referred to in subsection (a) (1).

(c) SUMMONS TO WHICH SECTION APPLIES. —

(1) IN GENERAL. — Except as provided in paragraph (2), a summons is described in this subsection if it is issued under paragraph (2) of section 7602 or under section 6420 (e) (2), 6421 (f) (2), 6424 (d) (2), or 6427 (e) (2) and requires the production of records.

(2) EXCEPTIONS. — A summons shall not be treated as described in this subsection if —
(A) it is solely to determine the identity of any person having a numbered account (or similar arrangement) with a bank of other institution described in subsection (a) (3) (A), or (B), or if it is in aid of the collection of —
(i) the liability of any person against whom an assessment has been made or judgment rendered, or
(ii) the liability at law or in equity of any transferee or fiduciary or any person referred to in clause (i).

(3) RECORDS: CERTAIN RELATED TESTIMONY. — For purposes of this section —
(A) the term 'records' includes books, papers, or other

data, and

(B) a summons requiring the giving of testimony relating to records shall be treated as a summons requiring the production of records.

(d) RESTRICTION ON EXAMINATION OF RECORDS. — No examination of any records required to be produced under a summons as to which notice is required under subsection (a) may be made

   (1) before expiration of the 14-day period allowed for the notice not to comply under subsection (b) (2), or
   (2) when the requirements of subsection (b) (2) have been met, except in accordance with an order issued by a court of competent jurisdiction authorizing examination of such records or with the consent of the person staying compliance.

(e) SUSPENSION OF STATUTE OF LIMITATIONS. — If any person takes any action as provided in subsection (b) and such person is the person with respect to whose liability the summons is issued . . . then the running of the period of limitations under section . . . 6531 (relating to criminal prosecutions) with respect to such person shall be suspended for the period during which a proceeding, and appeals thereto, with respect to the enforcement of such summons, is pending.

(f) ADDITIONAL REQUIREMENT IN THE CASE OF A JOHN DOE SUMMONS. — Any summons described in subsection (c) which does not identify the person with respect to whose liability the summons is issued may be served only after a court proceeding in which the Secretary establishes —

   (1) the summons relates to the investigation of a particular person or ascertainable group or class of persons,
   (2) there is a reasonable basis for believing that such person or group or class of persons may fail or may

have failed to comply with any provision of any internal revenue law, and

(3) the information sought to be obtained from the examination of the records (and the identity of the person or persons with respect to whose liability the summons is issued) is not readily available from other sources.

(g) SPECIAL EXCEPTION FOR CERTAIN SUMMONSES. — In the case of any summons described in subsection (c), the provisions of subsection (a) (1) and (b) shall not apply if, upon petition by the Secretary, the court determines, on the basis of the facts and circumstances alleged, that there is reasonable cause to believe the giving of notice may lead to attempts to conceal, destroy, or alter records relevant to the examination, to prevent the communication of information from other persons through intimidation, bribery, or collusion, or to flee to avoid prosecution, testifying, or production of records.

(h) JURISDICTION OF DISTRICT COURT. —

(1) The United States district court for the district within which the person to be summoned or is found shall have jurisdiction to hear and determine proceedings brought under subsection (f) and (g). The determinations required to be made under subsections (f) and (g) shall be made ex parte and shall be made solely upon the petition and supporting affidavits. An order denying the petition shall be deemed a final order which may be appealed.

(2) Except as to cases the court considers of greater importance, a proceeding brought for the enforcement of any summons, or a proceeding under this section, and appeals, take precedence on the docket over all cases and shall be assigned for hearing and decided at the earliest practicable date.

SUPREME COURT DECISIONS

THE RIGHT OF ANY TAXPAYER OR LITIGANT TO REPRESENT HIMSELF IN ANY COURT PROCEEDING.

Faretta v. California 421 US 806 (June 30, 1975):

(This involves a case in which Faretta demanded the right to conduct his own defense, which the lower court refused):

"The colonists brought with them an appreciation of the virtues of self-reliance and a traditional distrust of lawyers. When the Colonies were first settled, 'the lawyer was synonymous with the cringing attorneys-general and Solicitors-General of the Crown and the arbitrary Justices of the King's Court, all bent on the conviction of those who opposed the King's prerogatives, and twisting the law to secure convictions.' This prejudice gained strength in the colonies where . . . Virginia, Connecticut, and the Carolinas prohibited pleading for hire in the 17th century . . . The years of Revolution and confederation saw an upsurge of anti-lawyer sentiment . . . In the heat of these sentiments, the Constitution was forged."

(In England, before 1641, when Parliament abolished the Star Chamber Courts, the) "defendants were not only allowed counsel, but were required to get their answers signed by counsel. The effect of this was that no defense could be put before the Court which counsel would not take the responsibility for signing — a responsibility which, at that time, was extremely serious...

"The language and spirit of the Sixth Amendment contemplates that counsel, like the other defense tools guaranteed by the Amendment, shall be an aid to a willing defendant — and not an organ of the State interposed between an unwilling defendant and his right to defend himself personally. To thrust counsel upon the accused, against his considered wish, thus violates the logic of the Amendment. In such a case, counsel is not an assistant, but a master; and the right to make a defense is stripped of the personal character upon which the Amendment insists . . . An unwanted counsel 'represents' the defendant only through a tenuous and unacceptable legal fiction. Unless the accused has acquiesced in such representation, the defense presented is not the defense guaranteed him by the Constitution, for, in a very real sense, it is not *his* defense."

". . . in all courts, all persons of all persuasions may freely appear in their own way, and, according to their own manner, and there personally plead their own cause themselves; or, if unable, by their friends . . ."

(Does this not imply that such defense may be presented by persons who are not licensed attorneys or members of the bar?)

THE PROHIBITION AGAINST ANY GOVERNMENT AGENCY FROM ASSESSING AN ADDITIONAL TAX-LIABILITY SIMPLY BECAUSE TAXPAYER DECLINES TO SHOW RECORDS.

Boyd v. United States 116 US 616 (Feb. 1, 1886):
FROM THE SYLLABUS
"The 5th Section of the Act of June 28, 1874 . . . authorizes a court of the United States, in revenue cases, on motion of the government attorney, to require the defendant or claimant to produce in court his private books, invoices, and papers or else the allegations of the attorney to be taken as confessed: *Held*, To be unconstitutional and void . . .

"It does not require actual entry upon premises and search for and seizure of papers to constitute an unreasonable search and seizure within the meaning of the Fourth Amendment . . .

"It is equivalent to a compulsory production of papers, to make the non-production of them a confession of the allegations which it is pretended they will prove.

"A proceeding to forfeit a person's goods for an offense against the laws, though civil in form, and whether *in rem* or *in personam*, is a "criminal case" within the meaning of that part of the Fifth Amendment which declares that no person "shall be compelled, in any criminal case, to be a witness against himself."

"The seizure or compulsory production of a man's private papers to be used in evidence against him is equivalent to compelling him to be a witness against himself, and, in a

prosecution for a crime, penalty or forfeiture, is equally within
the prohibition of the Fifth Amendment ...
  "Both amendments relate to the personal security of the
citizen. They nearly run into and throw light upon each other.
When the thing forbidden in the Fifth Amendment, namely,
compelling a man to be a witness against himself, is the object of
a search and seizure of his private papers, it is an "unreasonable search and seizure" within the Fourth Amendment.
  "Constitutional provisions for the security of person and
property should be liberally understood."

FROM THE OPINION OF THE COURT
  "On the trial of the cause it became important to show the
quantity and value of the glass contained in the twenty-nine cases
previously imported. To do this, the district attorney offered in
evidence an order made by the District Judge under #5 of the
same Act of June 22, 1874, directing notice under seal of the court
to be given to the claimants, requiring them to produce the
invoice of the twenty-nine cases. The claimants, in obedience to
the notice, but objecting to its validity and to the constitutionality
of the law, produced the invoice; and when it was offered in
evidence by the district attorney they objected to its reception on
the ground that, in a suit for forfeiture, no evidence can be
compelled from the claimants themselves, and also that the
statute, so far as it compels production of evidence, to be used
against the claimants, is unconstitutional and void (618)...
  "As the question raised ... is a very grave question of constitutional law, involving the personal security, and privileges and
immunities of the citizen, we will set forth the order at large ...
(618)
  "The 5th section of the Act of June 22, 1874 . . . is in the
following words, to wit:
  " 'In all suits and proceedings other than criminal arising
under any of the revenue laws of the United States, the attorney
representing the government, whenever in his belief any
business book, invoice, or paper belonging to, or under the
control of, the defendant or claimant, will tend to prove any
allegation made by the United States, may ... issue a notice to

the defendant or claimant to produce such book, invoice, or paper in court . . .; and if the defendant or claimant shall fail or refuse to produce such book, invoice, or paper in obedience to such notice, the allegations stated in such motion shall be taken as confessed . . . And if produced, the said attorney shall be permitted, under the direction of the court, to make examination . . . of such entries in said book, invoice, or paper as relate to or tend to prove the allegations aforesaid, and may offer the same in evidence on behalf of the United States' . . . (619-20)

"The clauses of the Constitution, to which it is contended that these laws are repugnant, are the Fourth and Fifth Amendments . . . in regard to the Fourth Amendment, it is contended that . . . the order in the present case . . . is free from constitutional objection, because it does not authorize the search and seizure of books and papers, but only requires the defendant or claimant to produce them. That is so; but it declares that if he does not produce them, the allegations which it is affirmed they will prove shall be taken as confessed. This is tantamount to compelling their production . . . It is true that certain aggravating incidents of actual search and seizure, such as forcible entry into a man's house and searching amongst his papers, are wanting . . .; but it accomplishes the substantial object of these acts in forcing from a party evidence against himself. It is our opinion, therefore, that a compulsory production of a man's private papers to establish a criminal charge against him, or to forfeit his property, is within the scope of the Fourth Amendment to the Constitution, in all cases in which a search and seizure would be; because it is a material ingredient, and effects the sole object and purpose of search and seizure.

"The principal question, however, remains to be considered. In a search and seizure, or, what is equivalent thereto, a compulsory production of a man's private papers, to be used in evidence against him in a proceeding to forfeit his property for alleged fraud against the revenue laws — is such a proceeding for such a purpose an *unreasonable* search and seizure' within the meaning of the Fourth Amendment to the Constitution? or is it a legitimate proceeding? . . . (621-22)

"It is not the breaking of his doors, and the rummaging of

his drawers, that constitute the essence of the offence; but it is
the invasion of his indefeasible right of personal security,
personal liberty, and private property . . . In this regard the
Fourth and Fifth Amendments run almost into each other . . .
(629-30)

"Reverting to the peculiar phraseology of the Act, and to the
information in the present case, which is founded on it, we have to
deal with an act which expressly excludes criminal proceedings
from its operation (through embracing civil suits for penalties
and forfeitures), and with an information not technically a
criminal proceeding, and neither, therefore, within the literal
form of the Fifth Amendment to the Constitution any more than
it falls within the literal terms of the Fourth. Does this relieve the
proceedings or the law from being obnoxious to the prohibitions
of either? — We think not; we think they are within the spirit of
both.

"We have already noticed the intimate relation between the
two amendments. They throw light on each other. For the
"unreasonable searches and seizures" condemned in the Fourth
Amendment are almost always made for the purpose of
compelling a man to give evidence against himself, which in
criminal cases is condemned in the Fifth Amendment; and
compelling a man 'in a criminal case to be a witness against
himself,' which is condemned in the Fifth Amendment, throws
light on the question as to what is an 'unreasonable search and
seizure' within the meaning of the Fourth Amendment. And we
have been unable to perceive that the seizure of a man's private
books and papers to be used in evidence against him is
substantially different from compelling him to be a witness
against himself. We think it is within the clear intent and
meaning of these terms. We are also clearly of opinion that
proceedings instituted for the purpose of declaring the forfeiture
of a man's property by reason of offenses committed by him,
though they may be civil in form, are in their nature criminal . . .

"If the government prosecutor elects to waive an indictment,
and to file a civil information against the claimants — that is, in
civil form — can he by this device take from the proceeding its
criminal aspect and deprive the claimants of their immunities as

citizens, and extort from them a production of their private papers, or, as an alternative, a confession of guilt? This cannot be. The information, though technically a civil proceeding, is in substance and effect a criminal one ... (633-34)

"A witness, as well as a party, is protected by the law from being compelled to give evidence that tends to incriminate him, or to subject his property to forfeiture." (638)

COMMENTARY

We consider *Boyd v. United States* the most important of all Supreme Court decisions in the area of Fourth and Fifth Amendment rights. We know of no other opinion which states so clearly and specifically the immunities which our Founding Fathers placed in the Constitution to prevent for all future time any recurrence of the tyrannies they had suffered from a despotic and arbitrary government. If the IRS were to obey *Boyd*, it could never assess any deficiency because of a refusal to verify anything contained in an income-tax return. Should any Internal Revenue agent or other official declare that this has been superseded by later opinions, he should be told that every taxpayer has a right under *United States v. Bishop* to rely in good faith on *Boyd*; and that, if the Supreme Court has contradicted itself, we must then revert to the plain declarations of the Constitution.

It is therefore obvious that whenever an IRS agent assesses an increased tax simply because the taxpayer declines to produce records to verify deductions made under penalties of perjury, his action is infinitely more violative of the Constitution than were those of the officials in *Boyd*. In that case, a known smuggler — who had made no report at all — had evaded the import duty on a shipment of glass from Scotland. The government demanded that covering invoices be produced in court to determine the correct tax; or else that the smuggler be forced to pay whatever sum the customs officials might estimate to be due. The Supreme Court, however, declared that this procedure violated both the Fourth and the Fifth Amendments.

Publication 556

Examination of Returns, Appeal Rights, and Claims for Refund

1979 Edition

Department
of the
Treasury
Internal
Revenue
Service

Examination of Returns

Why Returns Are Selected for Examination

The usual reason for selecting a tax return for examination is to verify the correctness of income, exemptions, or deductions that have been reported on the return. Returns are primarily selected for examination by use of a computer program known as the Discriminant Function System (DIF). The DIF process is a mathematically based system that involves the assignment of weights to the entries on returns and the production by computer of a score for each return. The higher the score, the greater the probability of error in a return. Returns identified by DIF are then screened manually and those confirmed as having the highest error potential are selected for examination.

Returns may also be selected as part of the random sample under the Taxpayer Compliance Measurement Program (TCMP), which is the Service's long-range research program designed to measure and evaluate taxpayer compliance characteristics. Information obtained from TCMP is used to update and improve DIF.

The remaining returns are selected by other established selection methods, such as screening claims for refund of previously paid taxes and matching information documents (Forms W-2, 1099, and 1087).

The vast majority of taxpayers are honest and have nothing to fear from an examination of their tax returns. An examination of such a taxpayer's return does not suggest a suspicion of dishonesty or criminal liability. It may not even result in more tax. Many cases are closed without change in reported tax liability and in many others the taxpayer receives a refund.

Confidentiality of Tax Matters

You have the right to have your tax case kept confidential. The IRS has a duty under the law to protect the confidentiality of your tax information. However, if a lien or a lawsuit is filed, certain aspects of your tax case will become public knowledge.

The Internal Revenue Service has exchange agreements with state tax agencies under which information about any increase or decrease in tax liability on your state or federal return is shared with the other agency. If a federal tax return you have filed is changed, either by filing an amended return or as a result of being examined, it may affect your state income tax liability. It may be to your advantage to file an amended state tax return. Similarly, any change on your state income tax return may affect your federal return. Contact your state tax agency or the Internal Revenue Service for more information.

If Your Return Is Examined

The examination may be conducted by correspondence, or it may take place in your home or place of business, an Internal Revenue Service office, or the office of your attorney or accountant. The place and method of examination is determined by the Internal Revenue Service, but we try to select the place and method that is most appropriate under the circumstances, taking into account the complexity of your return. If the method is not convenient for you, we will attempt to work out something more suitable.

Whatever method of examination is used, you may act on your own behalf or you may have someone represent you or accompany you. An attorney, a certified public accountant, an individual enrolled to practice before the Internal Revenue Service, or the person who prepared the return and signed it as the preparer, may represent or accompany you.

If you prefer, you do not have to be present at a routine examination if you have authorized one of these persons to represent you. Authorization may be made on Form 2848-D, *Tax Information Authorization and Declaration of Representative*, which is available at any Internal Revenue Service office, or by means of any other properly written authorization.

If you filed a joint return, either you or your spouse, or both, may meet with us.

Transfers to Another District

As a general rule, the examination of a tax return is made in the Internal Revenue Service District where the taxpayer files. However, in any case where the examination of your return can be completed more quickly and conveniently in another district, you may request that the case be transferred to that district. Transfers are usually based on circumstances such as:

1) Your place of residence is changed before or during the examination; or
2) Your books and records are kept in another district.

The Examination

The examination normally begins when we notify you by mail that your return has been selected for examination. You will also be notified of the method of examination and the records you will need to assemble in order to clarify or prove items reported on your return. By assembling your records beforehand, you may be able to clear up questionable items or arrive at the correct tax with the least trouble.

Upon completion of the examination, our examiner will explain to you, or your authorized representative, any proposed change in your tax liability. The examiner will also explain the reasons for the change. It is important that you understand any proposed change, so please don't hesitate to ask questions about anything that is not clear to you. Most individual examinations are agreed to and closed at this level, but you don't have to agree and you may appeal any proposed change.

Repetitive Examinations

We try to avoid unnecessary repetitive examinations of the same items, but this occasionally happens. Therefore, if your tax return was examined in either of the 2 previous years for the same items and the examination resulted in no change to your tax liability, please contact the person whose name and telephone number are shown in the heading of the letter you received as soon as possible. The examination of your return will then be suspended pending a review of our files to determine whether it should proceed. However, if your return was selected for examination as part of the random sample for TCMP, discussed earlier, this procedure for exemption from examination will not apply and your return must be examined.

If You Agree

If you agree with the findings of the examiner, you will be asked to sign an agreement form. By signing, you will indicate your agreement to the amount shown on the form.

If you owe any additional tax, you may pay it when you sign the agreement. Interest is charged on the additional tax from the due date of your return to the date you pay.

If you do not pay the additional tax when you sign the agreement, you will be mailed a bill for the additional tax. Interest is charged on the additional tax from the due date of your return to the billing date. However, you will not be billed for more than 30 days interest from the date you sign the agreement. No further interest or penalties will be charged if you pay the amount you owe within 10 days after the billing date.

If the examination results in a refund, the Internal Revenue Service can refund your money more promptly if you sign the agreement form. You will receive interest at the applicable rate on the amount of the refund.

Appeal Rights

If You Don't Agree

If you don't agree with the changes proposed by the examiner, and if the examination was made in an Internal Revenue Service office, you may request an immediate meeting with a supervisor to explain your position. If agreement is reached, your case will be closed.

If agreement is not reached at this meeting, or if the unagreed examination was made outside of an Internal Revenue Service office, we will send you (1) a transmittal letter notifying you of your right to appeal the proposed adjustments within 30 days, (2) a copy of the examination report explaining the proposed adjustments, (3) an agreement or waiver form, and (4) a copy of Publication 5, *Appeal Rights and Preparation of Protests for Unagreed Cases.*

If after receiving the examination report you decide to agree with the examiner's findings, you should sign the agreement or waiver form. You may pay any additional amount you owe without waiting for a bill. Make your check or money order payable to the Internal Revenue Service. Include interest on the additional tax, but not on penalties, at the applicable rate from the due date of the return to the date of payment. Please do not send cash through the mail.

If after receiving the examination report you decide not to agree with the examiner's findings, we urge you to first appeal your case within the Service before you go to court.

Because people sometimes disagree on tax matters, the Service maintains an appeals system. Most differences can be settled within this system without having to go to court.

If you do not want to appeal your case in the Service, however, you can take it directly to court.

The following general rules tell you how to appeal your case.

Appeal Within the Service

We now have a single appeal level within the Service. Your appeal from the findings of the examiner is to the Appeals Office in the Region. Conferences are conducted on as informal a basis as is possible.

If you want an appeals conference, address your request to your District Director in accordance with our transmittal letter to you. Your District Director will forward your request to the appeals office, which will arrange for a conference at a convenient time and place and will discuss the disputed issues fully with you or your representative. You or your representative should be prepared to discuss all disputed issues and to present your views at this meeting in order to save the time and expense of additional conferences. Most differences are resolved at this level.

If agreement is not reached at your appeals conference, you may, at any stage of the procedures, take your case to court. See *Appeals to the Courts,* later.

Written Protests

So that your case may get prompt and full consideration by the appeals officer, you may need to file a written protest with the District Director. You don't have to file a written protest, however, if:

1) The proposed increase or decrease in tax, or claimed refund, does not exceed $2,500 for any of the tax periods involved in field examination cases; or

2) Your examination was conducted by correspondence or by an interview at our office.

If a written protest is required, it must be submitted within the 30-day period granted in the letter transmitting the report of examination and should contain:

1) A statement that you want to appeal the findings of the examining officer to the Regional Director of Appeals;

2) Your name and address;

3) The date and symbols from the letter transmitting the proposed adjustments and findings you are protesting;

4) The tax periods or years involved;

5) An itemized schedule of the adjustments with which you do not agree;

6) A statement of facts supporting your position in any contested factual issue;

7) A statement outlining the law or other authority upon which you rely.

The statement of facts under (6) must be declared true under penalties of perjury. This may be done by adding to the protest the following signed declaration:

"Under the penalties of perjury, I declare that I have examined the statement of facts presented in this protest and in any accompanying schedules and statements and, to the best of my knowledge and belief, they are true, correct, and complete."

If your representative submits the protest for you, he or she may substitute a declaration stating:

1) That he or she prepared the protest and accompanying documents; and

3

2) Whether he or she knows personally that the statements of fact contained in the protest and accompanying documents are true and correct.

Representation

You may represent yourself at your appeals conference, or you may be represented by an attorney, certified public accountant, or an individual enrolled to practice before the Internal Revenue Service.

If your representative attends a conference without you, he or she may receive or inspect confidential information only in accordance with a properly filed power of attorney or a tax information authorization. Form 2848, *Power of Attorney and Declaration of Representative,* or Form 2848-D, *Tax Information Authorization and Declaration of Representative,* available from any Internal Revenue Service office, or any other properly written power of attorney or authorization may be used for this purpose.

You may also bring witnesses to support your position.

Appeals to the Courts

If you and the Service still disagree after your conference, or if you skipped our appeals system, you may take your case to the United States Tax Court, the United States Court of Claims, or your United States District Court. These courts are independent judicial bodies and have no connection with the Internal Revenue Service.

Tax Court

If your case involves a disagreement over whether you owe additional income tax, or estate or gift tax, or certain excise taxes of private foundations, public charities, and qualified pension plans, you may go to the United States Tax Court. To do this, ask the Service to issue a formal letter, called a *statutory notice of deficiency.* You have 90 days from the date this notice is mailed to you to file a petition with the Tax Court (150 days if addressed to you outside the United States).

The Tax Court hears cases only if the tax has not been assessed or paid. Therefore, you must be sure that your petition to the Court is timely filed. If it is not, the proposed liability will be automatically assessed against you. Once the tax is assessed, a notice of tax due (a bill) will be sent to you and you may no longer take your case to the Tax Court. You are then required by law to make payment within 10 days. If the tax remains unpaid after the 10-day period, the amount due will become subject to immediate collection. You should be aware that once the assessment has

been made, collection of the full amount due may proceed notwithstanding your belief that the assessment was excessive. Publication 586A, *The Collection Process,* is available at your local Internal Revenue Service office to explain our collection procedures.

If you filed your petition on a timely basis, the Court will schedule your case for trial at a location convenient to you. You may represent yourself before the Tax Court, or you may be represented by anyone admitted to practice before that Court.

If your case involves a dispute of $1,500 or less ($5,000 or less starting June 1, 1979) for any one taxable year, a simplified alternative procedure is provided by the Tax Court. Upon your request, and with the approval of the Tax Court, your case may be handled under the Small Tax Case procedures. At little cost to you in time or money, you can present your own case to the Tax Court for a binding decision. If your case is handled under this procedure, the decision of the Tax Court is final and cannot be appealed. You can obtain more information regarding the Small Tax Case procedures and other Tax Court matters from the United States Tax Court, 400 Second Street, N.W., Washington, D.C. 20217.

District Court and Court of Claims

Generally, the District Court and the Court of Claims hear tax cases only after you have paid the tax and have filed a claim for refund. As explained later under *Claims for Refund,* you may file a claim for refund if, after having paid your tax, you believe the tax is erroneous or excessive. If your claim is rejected, you will receive a statutory notice of disallowance of the claim. If we have not acted on your claim within 6 months from the date you filed it, you can then file suit for refund. A suit for refund must be filed not later than 2 years after we have disallowed your claim.

You may file your refund suit in your United States District Court or in the United States Court of Claims. You can obtain information about procedures for filing suit in either court by contacting the clerk of your District Court or the Clerk of the Court of Claims, 717 Madison Place, N.W., Washington, D.C. 20005.

1   IN THE UNITED STATES DISTRICT COURT

2   FOR THE DISTRICT OF ARIZONA

3

4   UNITED STATES OF AMERICA,

5   Plaintiff,

6   vs.   Civ. No. 78-687 Phx WEC
     MELVIN JOHNSON and
7   PEGGY J. JOHNSON,

8   Defendants

9

10

11   October 2, 1978
                                  10:00 a.m.
12   Courtroom No.1, Federal Bldg.
                                  Phoenix, Arizona 85025
13
            REPORTER'S TRANSCRIPT OF PROCEEDINGS
14
     BEFORE:
15
            HONORABLE WALTER E. CRAIG, Judge
16   U. S. District Court, Phoenix, Arizona

17   APPEARANCES:

18   MICHAEL JOHNS, ESQ.,
            Assistant United States Attorney
19
            IN PROPRIA PERSONA, for Defendant
20

21

22   Reported by:
                                  LLOYD V. WEYENBERG
23   Official Court Reporter
                                  U. S. District Court
24   Phoenix, AZ 85025
                                  253-9640
25

Appendix

2

```
 1                                    Phoenix, Arizona
 2                                    October 2, 1978
                                      10:00 o'clock a.m.
 3                                    Calendar
 4          THE CLERK:  Case No. Civil 78-687, Phoenix,
 5  United States of America versus Peggy J. Johnson, for
 6  hearing pursuant to Order that Respondent appear to show
 7  cause why she should not be compelled to appear and testify
 8  as commanded in IRS summons.
 9          MR. JOHNS:  Michael Johns, for the United States,
10  your Honor.  These two IRS summons enforcement cases.  The
11  Respondents have filed Responses in which they point out
12  that at the time they came in to comply with the Summons,
13  they wished to record the summons procedure in the event
14  they might wish to raise their Fifth Amendment rights.
15          We have gotten permission from the District
16  Director to allow them to bring in their recording devices,
17  and the IRS, in turn, will make their own recording, and
18  there will be a record, if they want to make a record on it,
19  and on that basis we would ask that the Summons be enforced.
20          THE COURT:  Do you understand what he said?
21          PEGGY JOHNSON:  I take it that we go ahead and
22  agree to give them what they want, then they will allow us
23  to have a tape recording, right?
24          THE COURT:  Right.
25          PEGGY JOHNSON:  And they, in turn, will have one
```

1   also.

2   MR. JOHNSON: That is what we originally told

3   them.

4   THE COURT: And you can also, at any time you

5   desire to, you cannot answer any questions based on your

6   privilege under the Fifth Amendment, if you care to do so.

7   PEGGY JOHNSON: This is what we care to do.

8   THE COURT: Very well.

9   There may be an Order requiring production of

10 the records and interviews, subject to the understanding the

11 Court has just announced.

12   MR. JOHNS: Yes, your Honor. I will put that in

13 the form of an Order and submit it this afternoon.

14   THE COURT: Very well.

15   THE CLERK: Would that be as to both cases? I

16 believe there is someone here on the second one for Mr.

17 Speiser.

18   MR. JOHNS: That is on the two Johnson cases.

19   THE COURT: Thank you.

20   THE CLERK: Case No. Civil 78- --

21   MR. JOHNSON: May I ask now where do we go from

22 here at this particular point?

23   In all honesty, I don't really trust the

24 Internal Revenue Department after the way I have been treated

25 and I put my trust in you and God, so I want to make a point

4

1	here --
2	THE COURT: I think your trust in God is safer.
3	MR. JOHNSON: Amen. Thomas Jefferson says, don't
4	trust man and the good of men, but bind him down with the
5	chains of the Constitution.
6	MR. JOHNS: Your Honor, the procedure we had in
7	mind is to simply send him a copy of the Order and then he
8	can go down and meet with the Revenue Officer.
9	THE COURT: When you get a copy of the Order in
10	the mail, then call the Internal Revenue Office and make an
11	appointment to go down with your equipment and your records.
12	MR. JOHNSON: Now, you say for myself to make an
13	appointment, because last time I was down there, he didn't
14	give me an opportunity. He said get down here with your
15	records. That is what I did, because I was scared to death
16	with these people. I don't have to be scared of them; only
17	God.
18	THE COURT: I don't blame you. When you receive
19	the copy of the Order in the mail, then you call the Internal
20	Revenue Office and tell them that pursuant to the Order of
21	the Court, you would like to make an appointment to go over
22	the records and answer any questions they care to propound to
23	you, or to take your Fifth Amendment privileges. And then
24	they will make you an appointment to go down and see them.
25	Okay?

1   MR. JOHNSON: Thank you.

2   THE COURT: Very well.

3   THE CLERK: Case No. --

4   PEGGY JOHNSON: May I ask a question?

5   THE COURT: Yes.

6   PEGGY JOHNSON: The fact that we are going to

7   claim our Fifth Amendment rights, don't we just claim our

8   Fifth Amendment rights today?

9   THE COURT: You better go down and find out what

10   they want to know first. Then you can take your Fifth

11   Amendment rights. You don't have to respond if you want to

12   take your Fifth Amendment rights.

13   PEGGY JOHNSON: When we went there, Mr. Morgan

14   got very upset, and I don't want him getting upset.

15   THE COURT: I am the Judge that is ruling on this

16   matter, and that is the ruling of the Court.

17   PEGGY JOHNSON: You are going to back it up, right?

18   THE COURT: He will comply with the Order.

19   PEGGY JOHNSON: Thank you, sir.

20   *   *   *

21

22

23

24

25

Appendix

ORIGINAL

1913   INTERNAL REVENUE INCOME TAX RETURN

TO BE FILLED IN BY COLLECTOR.

Form 1040.

TO BE FILLED IN BY INTERNAL REVENUE BUREAU.

List No. ....

.... District of . ...

Date received ....

INCOME TAX.

THE PENALTY
FOR FAILURE TO HAVE THIS RETURN IN
THE HANDS OF THE COLLECTOR OF
INTERNAL REVENUE ON OR BEFORE
MARCH 1 IS $20 TO $1,000.
(SEE INSTRUCTIONS ON PAGE 4.)

UNITED STATES INTERNAL REVENUE.

File No.   ....

Assessment List ....

Page .... Line ....

RETURN OF ANNUAL NET INCOME OF INDIVIDUALS.
(As provided by Act of Congress, approved October 3, 1913.)

RETURN OF NET INCOME RECEIVED OR ACCRUED DURING THE YEAR ENDED DECEMBER 31, 191___
(FOR THE YEAR 1913, FROM MARCH 1, TO DECEMBER 31.)

Filed by (or for) .... of ....
(Full name of individual.)   (Street and No.)

In the City, Town, or Post Office of .... State of ....
(Fill in pages 2 and 3 before making entries below.)

1. Gross Income (see page 2, line 12)......................................	$			
2. General Deductions (see page 3, line 7)	$			
3. Net Income	$			
Deductions and exemptions allowed in computing income subject to the normal tax of 1 per cent.				
4. Dividends and net earnings received or accrued, of corporations, etc., subject to like tax. (See page 2, line 11)..........	$			
5. Amount of income on which the normal tax has been deducted and withheld at the source. (See page 2, line 9, column A)..				
6. Specific exemption of $3,000 or $4,000, as the case may be. (See Instructions 3 and 19)				
Total deductions and exemptions. (Items 4, 5, and 6)........	$			
7. Taxable Income on which the normal tax of 1 per cent is to be calculated. (See Instruction 3).	$			

8. When the net income shown above on line 3 exceeds $20,000, the additional tax thereon must be calculated as per schedule below:

					INCOME.			TAX.		
1 per cent on amount over $20,000 and not exceeding $50,000....	$					$				
2 " " 50,000 " " 75,000....										
3 " " 75,000 " " 100,000....										
4 " " 100,000 " " 250,000....										
5 " " 250,000 " " 500,000....										
6 " " 500,000										
Total additional or super tax						$				
Total normal tax (1 per cent of amount entered on line 7)....						$				
Total tax liability....						$				

JEFFERSON ON BANKS, MONEY, AND INFLATION

Letter to John Taylor, May 28, 1816:

I sincerely believe, with you, that banking establishments are more dangerous than standing armies; and that the principle of spending money to be paid by posterity, under the name of funding, is but swindling futurity on a large scale.

The Second Eppes Letter, September 11, 1813:

If the debt which the banking companies owe be a blessing to anybody, it is to themselves alone, who are realizing a solid interest of eight or ten per cent on it. As to the public, these companies have banished all our gold and silver medium, which, before their institution, we had without interest, which never could have perished in our hands, and would have been our salvation in the hour of war; instead of which they have given us hundreds of millions of froth and bubble, on which we are to pay them heavy interest, until it shall vanish into air . . . . . .

The Third Eppes Letter, November 6, 1813:

When I speak comparatively of the paper emission of the old Congress and the present banks, let it not be imagined that I cover them with the same mantle. The object of the former was a holy one; for if ever there was a holy war, it was that which saved our liberties and gave us independence. The object of the latter, is to enrich swindlers at the expense of the honest and industrious part of the nation.

The sum of what has been said is . . . that specie is the most perfect medium, because it will preserve its own level; because, having intrinsic and universal value, it can never die in our hands, and it is the surest resource of reliance in time of war; . . . . that paper is liable to be abused, has been, is, and forever will be abused, in every country in which it is permitted; . . . that we are already at ten or twenty times the due quantity of medium, inasmuch that no man knows what his property is worth, because it is bloating while he is calculating . . . .

THE WISDOM OF LINCOLN AND JEFFERSON

"No men living are more worthy to be trusted than those who toil up from poverty, none less inclined to take or touch anything they have not honestly earned. Let them beware of surrendering a political power which they already possess, and which, if surrendered, will surely be used to close the door of advancement against such as they, and to fix disabilities and burdens upon them till all of liberty shall be lost.

Lincoln: Message to Congress, December 3, 1861

"Resolved, That the several States composing the United States ... are not united on the principle of unlimited submission to their general government; but that, by a compact under the style and title of a Constitution ... delegated to that government certain definite powers, reserving, each state to itself, the residuary mass of right to their own self-government; and that whensoever the general government assumes undelegated powers, its acts are unauthoritative, void, and of no force ....

".... free government is founded in jealousy, and not in confidence; it is jealousy and not confidence which prescribes limited constitutions ....

"In questions of power, then, let no more be heard of confidence in man, but bind him down from mischief by the chains of the Constitution."

Jefferson: *The Kentucky Resolutions*, 1798

"They, the people, and not the rich, are our dependence for continued freedom ....; we must not let our rulers load us down with perpetual debt .... If we run into such debts, as that we must be taxed in our meat and in our drink, in our necessaries and our comforts, in our labors and our amusements, for our callings and our creeds ..., our people ... must come to labor sixteen hours in the twenty-four, give the earnings of fifteen of these to the government ...; have ... no means of calling our mismanagers to account; ... And the forehorse of this frightful team is public debt. Taxation follows that, and in its train wretchedness and oppression."

Jefferson: Letter to Kercheval, July 12, 1816